Textiles reproduced in this book are in the permanent
collection of The Saint Louis Art Museum.

Cover: *Detail from a Kashmir shawl made in the late 19th century in India by a master weaver for export
to the West where they were very fashionable.*

Previous Page: *Pork Tenderloin (page 153)*

# The Artist In The Kitchen

A Cookbook by
The Saint Louis Art Museum

Continuing the tradition
of the first edition published in 1977.

PHOTOGRAPHS BY JON BRUTON STUDIOS

DESIGN BY OBATA DESIGN, INC.

# FOREWORD

The art of cooking, the art of serving, and the art of eating (to borrow M.F.K. Fisher's perfect phrase) have inspired artistic responses in every age and culture. *The Artist In The Kitchen* continues the tradition begun by a most successful first edition, published in 1977, and has evolved in cooking styles, tastes and design. You'll find in these pages favorites preserved from the first edition as well as many new recipes. We are most grateful to Phoebe Burke and Mary Morgan who have guided this project from its beginnings, directing its progress and driving its completion. We thank the many cooks, testers, and tasters. Their contributions of time, ingredients, and taste buds were generous. Special recognition goes to the Museum Shop staff under the direction of Rita Wells who managed the project. We appreciate the initial funding from the Bunge Corporation; their early faith in the cookbook was a great spark. Finally, we thank *you* for supporting our efforts at the Museum with your purchase of this book — I'm certain it will inspire many pleasant dining experiences for you, your family and friends.

*James D. Burke*

James D. Burke, Director

ISBN # 0-89178-039-4     Library of Congress Catalog Card Number 93-86013

# INTRODUCTION

*The Artist in the Kitchen is a cookbook for and by*

*The Saint Louis Art Museum community. It is a compendium of*

*recipes appropriate for family dining, yet suitable for entertaining.*

*The recipes emphasize the use of fresh, readily available*

*ingredients and current cooking techniques. They are generally*

*simple and easy to prepare, but often contain suggestions for*

*more sophisticated variations. The recipes reflect the nutrition*

*and health concerns of the 90s, yet eschew fads and trendiness.*

*This book is for the cook who takes pleasure in trying new recipes,*

*but savors the tried and true favorites.*

*We hope this book will serve as an inspiration*

*to the artist in your kitchen.  Enjoy!*

# ABOUT THE TEXTILE COLLECTION
## AT THE SAINT LOUIS ART MUSEUM

   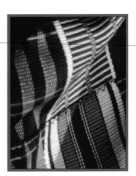

The Saint Louis Art Museum acquired its first textile in 1909. Early in this century it was recognized that the textile arts could teach much about technical, sociological, and artistic developments of the cultures in which they were produced. Since that time, the textile collection has grown to over 2,000 pieces that represent many cultures of the world and time periods. Among the earliest pieces in the collection are rare examples of ancient Peruvian weavings. Our strong holdings of Turkish rugs dating from the 15th century were given to the Museum by noted collector, James F. Ballard. Complementing these textiles is a fine collection of early Greek and Turkish embroideries. Textiles from Europe and North America include laces dating from the 16th century, the Carolyn C. McDonnell collection of fancy English needlework from the 17th and 18th centuries, as well as a representative collection of 19th and 20th century quilts and coverlets. The collections of Guatemalan and African textiles are other highlights among the Museum's textile holdings. And in keeping with the Museum's charter to collect the art of our time, we continue to collect contemporary fiber arts which reflect the highest artistic achievements from around the world.

# CONTENTS

**Butternut Soup**

(pg. 78)

**Cold Red Pepper and Tomato Gratin**

(pg. 87)

Grilled Chicken "Quatorze"

(pg. 121)

Orzo with Dilled Lemon Sauce
(pg. 169)

Chicken Provençal
*(pg. 125)*

**Grilled Tuna Steaks with Sun Dried Tomatoes and Fresh Corn**
(pg. 112)

Cravings Dark and White Chocolate Mousse Tart
*(pg. 196)*

**Apple Croustade**
(pg. 199)

# The RECIPES

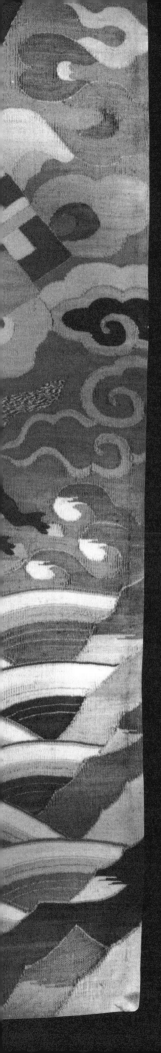

# APPETIZERS

Detail from one of a pair of 18th century

woven silk Chinese chair backs.

These decorative textiles were draped

over a chair for ceremonial purposes.

# CHEESE TWISTS

*These look very pretty placed in a basket lined with a colorful napkin.*

| | |
|---|---|
| 2 | sheets (1 package) puff pastry* |
| ½ | cup (1 stick) butter, melted |
| ½ | cup freshly grated Parmesan cheese |

Thaw pastry 20 minutes and unfold. Preheat oven to 425° F.

Brush each pastry sheet with butter and sprinkle with cheese. Press cheese gently into the pastry so it sticks. Cut into strips ½ inch wide x 10 inches long.

Place on baking sheet and twist each strip about 6 times. Bake for 15 to 20 minutes.

* Puff pastry can be found in frozen foods section of most supermarkets.

20

# CHEESE CRISPIES

| | |
|---|---|
| 1 | cup flour |
| ¼ | teaspoon salt |
| ¼ | teaspoon crushed red pepper flakes |
| ½ | cup (1 stick) unsalted butter, softened |
| 3 | cups (12 ounces) grated sharp Cheddar cheese |
| 1 | tablespoon chopped fresh thyme (or 1 teaspoon dried) |
| 1 | cup crisp rice cereal |

Preheat oven to 350° F. In a food processor, combine flour, salt and red pepper; pulse until blended. Add the butter, cheese and thyme and pulse just until a dough forms; bits of cheese should still be visible.

Transfer the dough to a large bowl and gently fold in the rice cereal. Working with a scant tablespoon at a time, roll the dough into balls.

Place the balls about 2 inches apart on ungreased cookie sheets. Flatten slightly with your fingertips into 1½-inch rounds.

Bake the crisps for about 15 minutes, or until firm to the touch and just beginning to brown. Let cool on the sheets for 1 to 2 minutes, then transfer to wire racks to cool completely.

Store in airtight containers for up to 1 day or freeze, well wrapped, for up to 1 month.

# CHEESE AND HERB COOKIES

MAKES ABOUT 30 COOKIES

1   cup flour

½   teaspoon baking powder

¼   teaspoon salt

⅓   cup butter, softened

¾   cup shredded Cheddar cheese

3   egg yolks

2   teaspoons water


FILLING

3   tablespoons butter, softened

1   teaspoon snipped fresh chives

¼   teaspoon dried oregano or basil

⅓   cup shredded Cheddar cheese

Salt and freshly ground pepper to taste

Paprika

Preheat oven to 400° F. Grease several baking sheets.

Sift flour, baking powder and salt into a medium-size bowl. Cut in butter until mixture resembles fine bread crumbs; mix in cheese. Add egg yolks and water; mix to form a dough.

Knead lightly on a floured surface until smooth. Roll out thinly. Prick well with a fork. Using a round 2-inch cookie cutter, cut out circles from dough and place on baking sheets.

Bake about 10 minutes or until lightly browned. Remove cookies to wire racks; cool.

**TO MAKE FILLING,** beat butter and chives in a small bowl until creamy. Beat in herbs and cheese. Season well with salt and pepper.

Sandwich cookies together with filling. Sprinkle lightly with paprika. Keep cool.

# CROSTINI

MAKES ABOUT 30 PIECES

1½ cups chopped or coarsely grated cheese
    such as Asiago, dry Jack or Mozzarella

½   cup coarsely chopped fresh basil

1   cup diced fresh tomatoes (peel, juice
    and seed before dicing)

3 to 5 cloves garlic, minced

½   cup coarsely chopped black
    Kalamata olives

2 or 3 baguettes (long narrow loaves of
French bread), sliced about ¼-inch thick

Combine cheese, basil, tomatoes, garlic and olives. This can be done several hours or a day before serving the Crostini.

Spread the mixture on the bread slices. Broil until lightly browned and bubbly, about 5 to 8 minutes. Serve immediately.

# JOSEPHINAS (a favorite from the original *Artist in the Kitchen*)

*A peppery twist on a cheese puff.*

French or sourdough bread, thinly sliced or pita triangles

1 cup (2 sticks) butter, softened

1 (4-ounce) can green chili peppers, chopped (hot, mild or half-and-half)

1 clove garlic, minced

1 cup mayonnaise

½ cup shredded Monterey Jack or Cheddar cheese

Toast bread slices on one side only. Combine and spread butter, chili peppers, and garlic on the untoasted sides.

Combine mayonnaise and cheese. Place a generous amount of mayonnaise-cheese mixture over butter mixture.

Broil until brown and bubbly. These may be made ahead and refrigerated before broiling.

# MUSHROOM AND ROQUEFORT STRUDELS

MAKES 16 MUSHROOMS

16 large, even-sized mushrooms

¼ pound Roquefort cheese, softened (or other softened blue cheese)

8 sheets phyllo pastry*

½ cup (1 stick) butter, melted

Salt and freshly ground pepper to taste

1 egg, beaten

Preheat oven to 400° F. Grease a baking sheet.

Wipe the mushrooms and carefully remove the stems. Fill the caps with Roquefort cheese.

Take out a sheet of phyllo (keeping others covered with a damp cloth so they don't dry out) and brush with butter. Place another sheet on top and brush with butter. Cut into 4 squares.

Put a filled mushroom in the center of each square and season with salt and pepper. Draw the edges of the pastry up together to look like a small sack. Pinch the "neck" together firmly with the fingers. Place on the baking sheet and brush with beaten egg. Repeat with the rest of phyllo.

Bake for 15 to 20 minutes until the pastry is golden brown. Serve immediately.

**Note:** *The strudels can be prepared, covered and refrigerated, but not baked, the day before.*

* *Packages of phyllo pastry are found in frozen foods section of most supermarkets. You will not use the whole package for this recipe.*

# Melted Brie with Winter Fruits

¾  cup chopped pitted dates

1  small apple, cored and diced

1  small firm ripe pear, cored and diced

½  cup currants

½  cup chopped pecans or walnuts

⅓  cup rosé wine or apple juice

1  (2-pound) round of ripe
Brie cheese, chilled

French bread, sliced thin, toasted if desired

In a bowl mix dates, fruit, nuts and wine or apple juice. Set aside to soften fruit, about 2 hours.

Cut Brie crosswise in half to make 2 round layers. Place 1 layer, cut side up, in attractive 10-inch shallow baking dish, such as a quiche pan. Make sure Brie fits serving dish snugly.

Spread cut side with 2½ cups fruit mix. Place remaining cheese layer, cut side down, on fruit. Spoon remaining fruit onto center of cheese.

Bake uncovered in 350° F. oven until cheese melts at edges and center is warm, about 15 to 20 minutes. Serve with French bread.

**Note:** *Brie can be prepared 2 days ahead and kept chilled until ready to bake.*

# Baked Camembert with Hazelnut Crust

SERVES 8 TO 10

1  (8-ounce) round of Camembert, the top rind cut away and discarded, leaving the bottom and side rind intact

1  egg, beaten lightly

¼  cup fine fresh bread crumbs

¼  cup finely chopped toasted and skinned hazelnuts (see page 205 for instructions)

Apple slices and toasted brioche or French bread as accompaniments

In a shallow dish coat the Camembert well on all sides with the egg.

In another shallow dish combine the bread crumbs and the hazelnuts.

Coat the Camembert well on all sides with the mixture, patting the mixture on to help it adhere. Chill on a plate, covered, for 1 hour.

Preheat oven to 400° F. Place the Camembert on a baking sheet, rindless side up, and bake for 15 minutes, or until the crust is golden brown. Transfer the Camembert carefully to a platter and serve it hot with apple slices and brioche.

# BRIE WITH HERBS IN BREAD

SERVES 6

*Try this for an elegant picnic!*

1   (10-ounce) baguette

¼   cup olive oil

3   tablespoons dry white wine

1   teaspoon coarsely ground black pepper

2   cloves garlic, minced

1   piece of ripe Brie cheese
    (about 10 ounces)

3   tablespoons snipped fresh chives

1   cup coarsely shredded fresh basil leaves

1½  cups coarsely shredded sorrel leaves
    (or other herbs, depending on availability)

Cut the baguette in half lengthwise. Blend the olive oil, wine, pepper and garlic in a small bowl. Drizzle over each baguette half, dividing evenly.

Trim the Brie to remove any crust and cut into ¼-inch slices, preferably large and thin.

Spread half the herbs on the cut surface of the bottom half of the loaf and arrange the cheese slices on top. Spread the remaining herbs on top of the Brie and place the top half of the bread loaf on top to reform the loaf.

Press firmly together and roll as tightly as possible in plastic wrap and then in aluminum foil. (If tightly wrapped, the bread absorbs the juices better.) Press the loaf between two baking sheets and refrigerate with 3 to 5 pounds of weight (a can or jar, perhaps) on top for 4 to 5 hours before cutting in slices to serve. It can be served cold or at room temperature.

24

# BAKED ALMONDS

2   cups whole blanched almonds

1   tablespoon olive oil

¼   teaspoon salt

¼   teaspoon sugar

Preheat oven to 400° F. Place almonds in a bowl and toss with oil to coat well. Scatter the almonds on a baking sheet. Roast for 15 to 20 minutes, tossing occasionally, until deep golden brown.

Remove from oven and sprinkle with salt and sugar and set aside to cool. Spread the cooled almonds on several layers of paper towels and blot them to remove excess oil. Almonds will keep 2 weeks in covered container.

# PEPPERED PECANS

1   *tablespoon olive oil*

1   *teaspoon freshly ground black pepper*

1   *teaspoon freshly ground white pepper*

1   *teaspoon cayenne pepper*

½   *teaspoon dried thyme, crumbled*

2   *egg whites*

1   *tablespoon Worcestershire sauce*

1   *tablespoon hot pepper sauce*

1   *teaspoon salt*

4¼ *cups pecan halves (about 1 pound)*

Position rack in upper third of oven and preheat to 375° F. Brush heavy large baking pan with oil.

Mix black and white pepper, cayenne pepper and thyme in small bowl. Whisk egg whites in medium bowl until foamy. Whisk in Worcestershire, hot pepper sauce and salt. Add pecans and toss to coat. Sprinkle pepper mixture over pecans, and toss again.

Spread pecan mixture evenly in prepared pan. Bake 5 minutes. Stir nuts, breaking up clumps. Bake until crisp and deep golden brown, stirring twice and watching carefully to prevent burning, about 7 minutes more. Transfer to bowl. Cool completely.

**Note:** *Pecans can be prepared several days ahead and stored in an airtight container.*

# CRISPY WONTONS

SERVES 8

SAUCE

1   *cup plum jelly*

½   *cup mango chutney*

1½ *tablespoons red wine vinegar*

1   *teaspoon dry mustard*

¼   *teaspoon hot pepper sauce*

1   *(14-ounce) package wonton skins*

*Vegetable oil (for deep frying)*

*3 or 4 scallions, chopped*

Combine jelly, chutney, vinegar, mustard and hot pepper sauce in heavy small saucepan. Stir over medium heat until thoroughly blended and bubbly. Spoon into bowl and set aside.

Cut wonton skins in half on diagonal.

Heat oil in deep fryer or deep skillet to 365° F. Add wonton skins in batches and fry until golden brown and blistered, 2 minutes. Drain on paper towels.

Garnish sauce with scallions. Serve hot or at room temperature with fried wonton skins.

# PHYLLO TRIANGLES WITH FETA AND SPINACH FILLING

*An excellent standard for the large cocktail party buffet.*
*Plan to make ahead as these are time consuming.*

1   pound (1 package) phyllo pastry*

⅓   cup olive oil

1   bunch scallions, chopped

2½  pounds spinach, washed and dried
    (or 2 (10-ounce) packages frozen
    chopped spinach)

1   bunch parsley, minced

1   bunch dill, minced

½   pound Feta cheese, drained and crumbled

3   eggs, lightly beaten

*Salt and freshly ground pepper to taste*

*2 to 3 sticks unsalted butter, melted*

Thaw phyllo overnight in the refrigerator, if frozen.

To make the filling, heat the olive oil and sauté the scallions until soft. Add the spinach and cook until wilted, stirring frequently.

Put the mixture in a colander over a bowl and press out the liquid. In a small saucepan, boil down the spinach liquid until it measures 2 tablespoons. Add this back to the spinach mixture, along with the parsley, dill, cheese and eggs and blend well. Season with salt and pepper and cool completely.

Preheat oven to 400° F. To assemble the triangles, place one sheet of phyllo on a flat surface and brush lightly with butter. (Keep rest of phyllo covered with a damp tea towel so it does not dry out.) Top this with two more sheets, buttering each. Cut the sheets in half lengthwise, then cut each half crosswise into 6 equal parts.

Spoon a teaspoon of filling onto the end of each strip and form a triangle by folding the right-hand corner to the opposite side, as you would a flag. Continue folding until the entire strip is used.

Place triangles on a buttered baking sheet. Brush the tops of each with melted butter and bake until golden brown, about 10 minutes.

**Note:** *Filled phyllo triangles can be covered tightly and refrigerated, unbaked, for 2 days, or frozen immediately for future use.*

* *Packages of phyllo pastry are found in frozen foods section of most supermarkets. You will not use the whole package for this recipe.*

26

# BAKED WHOLE HEADS OF GARLIC

SERVES 6

1 to 2 tablespoons olive oil

6   heads of garlic

½   teaspoon dried thyme
    (or a few fresh sprigs)

½   teaspoon chopped fresh rosemary

Freshly ground pepper to taste

Preheat oven to 350° F. Cut a large double thick square of aluminum foil and brush with some of the olive oil. Place the garlic heads on the foil and brush the garlic with remaining olive oil and sprinkle with the herbs and pepper. Fold the foil up over the garlic and crimp the edge together tightly, leaving some space around the garlic.

Bake about 1 to 1½ hours until the garlic is very soft. Remove from the foil and cool to room temperature. Separate into individual cloves or clumps of a few cloves. Squeeze cloves onto toast or french bread, or serve with a roast or any grilled meat. ▨

# BACON-WRAPPED SCALLOPS

SERVES 6

15 large sea scallops, halved, rinsed
   and patted dry

10 slices bacon

## MARINADE

¼   cup bourbon

¼   cup soy sauce

¼   cup Dijon mustard

¼   cup minced scallions

¼   cup brown sugar

½   teaspoon Worcestershire sauce

Freshly ground pepper to taste

Combine marinade ingredients and pour over scallops. Let them marinate for 1 hour, tossing occasionally. Remove from marinade with a slotted spoon.

Cut bacon crosswise into thirds. Wrap a piece of bacon around each scallop and thread scallops onto metal skewers, leaving ¼-inch between each scallop.

Grill or broil for 3 to 5 minutes. Turn twice and cook until bacon is crisp. Gently remove from skewers. ▨

# COUNTRY PÂTÉ

SERVES 8

½  cup Madeira

½  cup brandy

½  pound chicken livers

½  pound ground veal

¾  pound sliced bacon

4  tablespoons (½ stick) butter, divided

1  medium onion, chopped (½ cup)

1  pound ground pork

⅛  teaspoon ground cloves

⅛  teaspoon ground nutmeg

¼  teaspoon minced fresh ginger

Salt and freshly ground pepper to taste

2  cloves garlic, minced

2  eggs

½  cup heavy cream

½  cup shelled pistachios

½  pound cooked ham, thickly sliced

1  bay leaf

The night before cooking the pâté, mix the Madeira and brandy in a medium bowl. Add the chicken livers and veal. Cover and refrigerate overnight.

When ready to cook, preheat oven to 350° F. Line a terrine or loaf pan with bacon. Melt 2 tablespoons butter and sauté onion until soft. Set aside.

With a slotted spoon lift the livers and veal out of Madeira-brandy mixture (reserving the liquid) and place in a food processor along with the cooked onion, pork, cloves, nutmeg, ginger, salt and pepper. Blend until smooth. Add garlic, eggs, cream and ½ cup of reserved Madeira-brandy mixture.

Cut the ham in strips and quickly sauté in remaining butter until they shrink a little. Spread a third of the pâté mixture in the terrine. Lay half of the ham strips over. Spread half of the remaining pâté, cover with the rest of the ham strips and end with pâté. Lay the bay leaf on top, sprinkle a few teaspoons of remaining Madeira-brandy mixture over and cover with lid if using terrine or with aluminum foil if using a loaf pan.

Place terrine in a larger pan with several inches of hot water and cook for 1½ hours. Cool. Remove the lid if using and press top with a 2-pound weight for at least 3 hours while refrigerated. To serve, slice thinly and serve with sliced baguettes.

**Note:** *This pâté tastes even better after 3 days as flavors have had a chance to meld. It keeps for at least a week refrigerated and also can be frozen.*

# Spiced Tortellini on Skewers

SERVES 8 TO 10

1 (9-ounce) package cheese or
   spinach tortellini

3 to 5 tablespoons olive oil

1 tablespoon hot red pepper flakes

¼ cup freshly grated Parmesan cheese

Cook tortellini according to package instructions and drain well. While still hot, roll in a little olive oil, then sprinkle with hot red pepper. Let cool and set aside, covered. Right before serving, roll tortellini in Parmesan cheese and place in serving dish with wooden skewers or extra long toothpicks. ▨


# Barbecued Pork Strips

SERVES 8

*A very desirable addition to a cocktail buffet.*

2 or 3 pork tenderloins

MARINADE

2½ tablespoons honey

2 tablespoons soy sauce (or more to taste)

1 tablespoon dry sherry

1 large clove garlic, minced

1 small piece fresh ginger, minced

2 tablespoons hoisin sauce* (optional)

1 tablespoon oriental sesame oil* (optional)

Place the tenderloins in a shallow glass or ceramic dish. Mix the ingredients for the marinade and pour over, turning to coat well. Cover and let marinate 2 to 3 hours before cooking.

When ready to cook, remove meat from dish, reserving marinade for basting. For oven roasting, put the meat on a rack in a roasting pan containing some water. Roast in a preheated 425° F. oven for 10 minutes. Baste meat with the reserved marinade, reduce oven to 350° and roast 25 to 30 minutes more. Baste meat at 10-minute intervals, turning if desired.

For charcoal grilling, cook the marinated pork over medium hot coals, allowing 15 minutes per side. If you cook them with the grill cover closed, 10 minutes per side may be enough. Turn and baste as above, and watch carefully to avoid charring or flaming.

To serve, slice pork against the grain into thin rounds and serve hot or cold on sliced baguettes or pumpernickel. Pork can be accompanied by a hot honey mustard sauce or a mixture of sesame oil and hoisin sauce. ▨

* Available in Oriental food section of most supermarkets.

# Tomato Salsa

3   large tomatoes, peeled, seeded, and
    coarsely chopped

⅓   cup chopped Spanish or red onion

½ to 1 teaspoon minced hot pepper,
    such as jalapeño

2   teaspoons minced garlic

Juice of 1½ limes

Salt and freshly ground pepper to taste

3   tablespoons chopped fresh cilantro

In a bowl combine tomatoes, onion, hot pepper, garlic, lime juice, salt and pepper to taste. Stir in cilantro and serve. Delicious with chips or serve with Mexican Quiche on page 31.

30

# Hummus bi Tahini (Chickpeas with Tahini)

½   cup fresh lemon juice (2 or 3 lemons)

¼   cup water

1½ to 2 cups canned chickpeas (garbanzos),
    drained

½   cup sesame tahini

2 or 3 cloves garlic, peeled

½   teaspoon red pepper (optional)

½   teaspoon salt (optional)

1   tablespoon olive oil

Paprika to taste

1   tablespoon cilantro or parsley, chopped

Combine lemon juice, water, chickpeas, tahini, garlic, red pepper and salt in a food processor or blender and mix to a paste the consistency of mayonnaise.

Spread the hummus in a shallow bowl. Drizzle with olive oil and sprinkle with paprika and chopped cilantro. Serve as a spread for warmed pita bread or a dip for fresh vegetables. ▣

# Mexican Quiche

SERVES 6

2   9-inch pie crusts

1   large onion, coarsely chopped (1 cup)

1   tablespoon butter or margarine

1   cup coarsely chopped tomato,
    drained and divided

1   (4-ounce) can sliced ripe olives,
    drained and divided

1   clove garlic, minced

¼   teaspoon ground cumin

⅛   teaspoon ground black pepper

1   (4-ounce) can chopped
    green chilies, drained

2   eggs, beaten

2 to 3 drops hot pepper sauce (to taste)

1   cup (4 ounces) shredded Monterey Jack
    cheese, divided

1   cup (4 ounces) shredded Cheddar
    cheese, divided

Sour cream

Salsa (see recipe page 30)

Preheat oven to 375° F. Place 1 crust in a 10-inch tart pan with removable bottom or in a 9-inch pie pan; press into bottom and up sides of pan. Trim edges, if necessary.

In medium skillet, sauté onions in butter until tender.

Reserve 1 tablespoon chopped tomato and 1 tablespoon sliced ripe olives. Stir remaining tomato, olives, garlic, cumin, black pepper and chilies into cooked onion.

In small bowl, beat eggs with hot pepper sauce; reserve 2 teaspoons of mixture.

Stir ½ cup Monterey Jack cheese and ½ cup Cheddar cheese into remaining egg mixture in bowl. Sprinkle remaining cheeses over bottom of pie crust. Spoon onion mixture evenly over cheese.

Carefully pour egg mixture over onion mixture; spread to cover. Top with second crust; seal edges. Slit crust in several places and brush with reserved egg mixture.

Bake on lowest rack in oven 45 to 55 minutes, or until golden brown. Let stand 5 minutes; remove sides of pan if using tart pan. Serve warm with sour cream, salsa and reserved chopped tomatoes and olives.

*31*

*Appetizers*

# WILD MUSHROOM TART

*An excellent first course to precede a light entrée of grilled fish or fowl, or serve it for a luncheon with a green salad and sliced tomatoes.*

## CRUST

1   cup flour

½   cup (1 stick) unsalted butter or margarine, room temperature, broken into pieces

5   tablespoons cold water

⅛   teaspoon salt

## FILLING

2   ounces dried porcini mushrooms* (or ½ pound fresh mushrooms, sliced)

¼   cup olive oil

2   tablespoons unsalted butter or margarine

1   medium red onion, finely chopped (½ cup)

15  sprigs Italian parsley, leaves only, finely chopped

1   cup beef broth (homemade or canned) (if using fresh mushrooms)

Salt and freshly ground pepper to taste

3   eggs, beaten lightly

½   cup freshly grated Parmesan cheese

**TO PREPARE CRUST,** sift flour into a bowl. Cut butter into flour with fingers or pastry blender. Sprinkle in water and salt and mix with a fork. Form a ball of dough with your hands. Knead gently until dough becomes very smooth (about 2 minutes). Wrap dough in a slightly dampened tea towel or wax paper. Refrigerate at least 1 hour.

**TO PREPARE FILLING,** soak dried mushrooms in 1 cup of warm water for about ½ hour. Heat oil and butter in a heavy saucepan and, when the butter is completely melted, add the onion, parsley and fresh mushrooms if using. Sauté gently for about 10 minutes. Lift the porcini mushrooms out of the warm water and rinse and pat dry. Strain the mushroom liquid (a paper coffee filter works well). Add mushrooms to pan and sauté for 5 minutes, stirring occasionally. Add mushroom liquid (or beef broth), salt and pepper. Cook slowly until most of the broth has evaporated and filling is thick, about 35 minutes. Remove pan from heat and transfer filling to a crockery or glass bowl and cool completely.

**TO ASSEMBLE TART,** butter 9½-inch tart pan with a removable bottom. Unwrap dough and knead it on a floured board for 1 minute, roll out to a 14-inch round. Transfer to tart pan and gently press into pan. Trim edges and puncture pastry with fork to prevent bubbles from forming. Fit a round of wax paper or aluminum foil over pastry and fill with dried beans or pastry weights. Refrigerate for ½ hour. Preheat oven to 375° F. Bake crust for 40 minutes, remove beans or weights, and bake for an additional 10 to 15 minutes. Meanwhile, to finish the filling, add the eggs and Parmesan cheese to cooled mushroom mixture. After the crust has cooled about 10 minutes, add filling and bake for 20 minutes. Cool for 15 minutes before transferring to serving platter. Serve at room temperature.

*\* Available in specialty food stores.*

# PISSALADIÈRE

MAKES 16 PIECES

*A lighter version of pizza.*

2   sheets (1 package) puff pastry*

2 or 3 tomatoes, thinly sliced

Freshly ground pepper to taste

¾   cup coarsely chopped imported
      black olives (Kalamata or Italian)

1   (4-ounce) can anchovy fillets

1   egg, beaten

Fresh chopped basil

Thaw pastry 20 minutes and unfold. Preheat oven to 400° F. Cut four 5-x-6-inch rectangles from the pastry sheets. Place on baking sheet. Cut remaining pastry into ½-inch strips and place along edges of rectangles to form raised borders. Prick centers of pastry with a fork.

Arrange tomato slices in rows on top overlapping slightly. Sprinkle with pepper. Place olives and anchovies on top. Brush borders with egg. Bake for 10 to 15 minutes. After removing from oven, cut each rectangle into 4 triangles. Sprinkle with basil.

* Puff pastry can be found in frozen foods section
  of most supermarkets.

# RED PEPPER MOUSSE

MAKES 2 CUPS

*Serve alone or as accompaniment to cold roasted meats.*

1   teaspoon olive oil

1   teaspoon butter

4   red bell peppers, cut into ¼-inch dice

1   medium clove garlic, minced

⅛   teaspoon dried thyme

1   tablespoon white wine vinegar

⅔   cup heavy cream, whipped

¼   teaspoon freshly ground white pepper

Salt to taste

Toasted rounds of French bread

Melt olive oil and butter in heavy medium saucepan over low heat. Add peppers, garlic and thyme. Cover and cook over low heat, stirring occasionally to prevent burning, about 20 minutes.

Add vinegar, increase heat to medium and cook, uncovered, until all liquid has evaporated. Transfer mixture to blender or food processor and mix 30 seconds. Cool completely.

Gently fold pepper purée into whipped cream. Season mousse with pepper and salt and serve with French bread.

# TOMATO HERB TART

*Bright colors and robust flavors make this tart a great addition to any meal — as a first course, a side dish for a simple entrée or a luncheon dish.*

## PASTRY CRUST*

1½  cups unbleached flour

½   cup finely ground toasted almonds

1   tablespoon brown sugar

¼   teaspoon salt

⅔   cup (1 stick plus 3 tablespoons) unsalted butter

## FILLING

2   tablespoons Dijon mustard

1   cup grated Mozzarella cheese

8 or 9 medium pear-shaped Italian tomatoes, sliced ¼-inch thick

2   tablespoons extra virgin olive oil, divided

3   tablespoons minced garlic

¼   cup chopped fresh parsley

¼   cup chopped fresh basil

3   tablespoons freshly grated Asiago, Parmesan or Romano cheese

Salt and freshly ground pepper to taste

Preheat oven to 350° F. To make pastry, thoroughly mix flour, almonds, brown sugar and salt. Cut butter into mixture with fingers or pastry blender until crumbly. Work dough into a ball, wrap well and refrigerate for at least 1 hour.

Press pastry into 10-inch tart pan or 9-inch pie pan until even and smooth. Prick bottom with a fork and bake for 5 to 7 minutes until lightly browned. Remove from oven and cool.

Spread mustard evenly over pastry and sprinkle with Mozzarella. Evenly layer tomatoes in a spiral pattern starting from the outside working toward the center.

Sauté garlic until just softened in 1 tablespoon olive oil. Mix with parsley, basil, remainder of olive oil, Asiago cheese, salt and pepper. Sprinkle evenly over tomatoes. Bake for 25 to 35 minutes until top is evenly browned. Cool and serve at room temperature.

*\* You can substitute commercially prepared pie crust available in the dairy section of the supermarket.*

# HOT SPICY SHRIMP

SERVES 4

*Serve as an appetizer on little plates or as a first course.*

1   medium red bell pepper, roasted, peeled and seeded

¼   cup olive oil, divided

1½  pounds large shrimp, peeled, deveined, rinsed and patted dry

3   tablespoons minced fresh ginger

2   garlic cloves, minced

1½  tablespoons fresh lemon juice

1   tablespoon fresh lime juice

¼   teaspoon salt

½   teaspoon Chinese hot (red chili) oil

¼   cup snipped fresh chives or scallion greens

Prepare roasted pepper according to instructions on page 75. Peel, seed, mince and set aside.

In a large heavy skillet, heat 2 tablespoons of the oil over high heat. Add shrimp and cook, turning, until opaque and firm, about 2 to 3 minutes. Transfer shrimp to a medium bowl and set aside to cool.

Reduce heat to moderately low and add ginger and garlic. Cook, stirring, until fragrant and starting to soften, about 3 minutes.

Scrape the ginger mixture into a small bowl and whisk in lemon juice, lime juice and salt. Whisk in the remaining 2 tablespoons olive oil and the hot oil. Pour mixture over the cooled shrimp, stir to coat and let sit for at least 1 hour. Stir in chives and minced red pepper before serving.

**Note:** *The shrimp can be prepared 1 day ahead and refrigerated. Bring to room temperature for 1 hour and add chives and red pepper before serving.*

# BREADS

Detail of mid 19th century American quilt

designed with large repeating motifs and

bold borders which are typical of this period.

# BRAN MUFFINS

½   cup boiling water

1¼  teaspoons baking soda

½   cup raisins or currants

1   cup bran flakes

½   cup (1 stick) butter

½   cup sugar

⅓   cup dark molasses

1   egg

1   cup buttermilk

1¼  cups flour

¼   teaspoon salt

1⅓  cups oat bran

Preheat oven to 400° F. Mix together boiling water, baking soda, raisins and bran flakes. Set aside.

In another bowl, beat together butter, sugar and molasses until creamy. Add egg, then buttermilk, beating well after each addition.

Add flour, salt, oat bran and raisin mixture and blend well. Fill paper-lined muffin cups ⅔ full and bake for 20 minutes.

*Note: Recipe doubles well and can be stored in refrigerator up to 2 weeks.*

38

# BANANA MUFFINS

1   teaspoon baking soda

4   tablespoons buttermilk

1½  cups flour

¼   teaspoon salt

½   cup (1 stick) butter

1   cup sugar

2   eggs

2   bananas, mashed

1   teaspoon vanilla

Preheat oven to 375° F. Stir soda into buttermilk and let stand until foamy. Sift together flour and salt and set aside.

In a medium-sized bowl, cream butter and sugar. Blend in eggs, one at a time, and then the mashed bananas. Alternately, add flour and buttermilk mixture and vanilla, blending gently until just mixed.

Spoon into greased or paper-lined muffin cups. Fill until ⅔ full. Bake for about 20 minutes, until nicely browned.

*Note: 1 teaspoon poppy seeds or ¼ teaspoon freshly grated nutmeg may be added for variation.*

# "A" IS FOR APPLE MUFFINS

MAKES 12 MUFFINS

*Most muffins taste best within minutes after coming out of the oven, but these beauties stay fresh for several days if kept well-wrapped in the refrigerator. They also freeze very well. The goodness and natural sweetness of these fiber rich muffins come from the fruit. Heavy stiff batter is more like a fruitcake than a muffin.*

2  cups apples, peeled and chopped
   (Jonathans or Granny Smiths are best)

½  cup sugar (or less to taste)

1  egg, lightly beaten

¼  cup vegetable oil

1  teaspoon vanilla extract

1  cup flour

1  teaspoon baking soda

1  teaspoon cinnamon

½  teaspoon salt

½  cup raisins

½  cup dried apricots, diced

⅓  cup sweetened shredded coconut
   (optional)

Preheat oven to 350° F. Grease 12 muffin tins, or use spray or cup liners.

Mix apples with sugar and set aside. In another bowl beat egg lightly and blend with oil and vanilla. Pour egg mixture over apples and sugar and blend thoroughly.

In another bowl, mix flour with baking soda, cinnamon and salt. Sprinkle flour mixture over apple mixture and mix well using hands or a large spoon. Batter is lumpy and thick. Add raisins, apricots and coconut, mixing well. Using ¼ cup measure, fill muffin tins.

Bake about 20 minutes or until golden brown. Serve warm. These muffins have an almost glazed top. 

**Variations:** *Instead of ⅓ cup coconut substitute ⅓ cup chopped walnuts, pecans or almonds. Omit apricots and substitute 1 finely grated carrot.*

# RITZY BLUEBERRY MUFFINS

MAKES 12 MUFFINS

1¾ cups flour

1 tablespoon baking powder

½ cup sugar

2 eggs, slightly beaten

⅓ cup milk

6 tablespoons (¾ stick) butter, melted and cooled

½ teaspoon vanilla

2 cups fresh blueberries or 1 (12-ounce) bag frozen

Sugar to sprinkle on top

Preheat oven to 400° F. Mix all dry ingredients. Stir in eggs, milk, butter and vanilla. Do not over mix. Carefully fold in berries.

Spray top of muffin tin with vegetable spray. Insert paper cups in tin and spoon batter to top of paper cups. Sprinkle generously with sugar.

Place muffin tin in middle rack in oven and bake 20 to 25 minutes until golden brown.

40

# RHUBARB MUFFINS

MAKES 8 TO 12 MUFFINS

*Rhubarb is tart, flavorful and healthy. These moist, not too sweet muffins are a favorite in early spring.*

2 cups diced fresh rhubarb

2 cups flour

2 teaspoons baking powder

¼ teaspoon salt

⅛ teaspoon ground cinnamon

1 egg

⅓ cup packed brown sugar

⅔ cup granulated sugar

3 tablespoons currant jelly, melted

1 cup milk

4 tablespoons (½ stick) butter, melted and cooled

½ teaspoon vanilla

Preheat oven to 400° F. Line muffin tins with paper cups.

Thoroughly mix flour, baking powder, salt and cinnamon in large bowl. In medium-sized bowl whisk egg, brown sugar, granulated sugar and currant jelly until smooth.

Add milk, butter and vanilla. Pour over flour mixture and fold lightly until dry ingredients are just moistened. Do not overmix. Fold in the rhubarb. Fill muffin cups to almost full.

Bake 20 to 25 minutes in middle of oven until tops are springy to touch and light brown. Cool in pan 5 minutes, then turn out onto cooling rack to finish cooling.

# ZUCCHINI NUT BREAD

2 cups zucchini, peeled

3 eggs

2 cups raw or brown sugar

2 cups flour

1 teaspoon baking soda

1 teaspoon baking powder

1½ teaspoons salt

2 teaspoons cinnamon

1 cup oil

2 teaspoons vanilla

1 cup chopped nuts (pecans or walnuts)

Preheat oven to 325° F. Grate zucchini and squeeze dry in a towel. Set aside.

Beat eggs until light; add sugar and beat. Sift and mix in dry ingredients. Fold into egg mixture. Add oil, zucchini, vanilla and nuts and mix well.

Pour into 2 large greased (not oiled) loaf pans.
Bake for 1 hour or until tester inserted in center comes out clean.

# DATE-NUT CAKE

MAKES 1 LOAF

*This luscious dark loaf-shaped cake is meltingly sweet and moist. A sliver will suffice.*

½ cup (1 stick) butter plus more for greasing pan

Flour

1 cup pitted and diced dates

½ cup dark raisins

½ cup golden raisins

1 teaspoon baking soda

1 cup boiling water

1 cup sugar

1 teaspoon vanilla

1 egg

1⅓ cups sifted flour

¾ cup walnuts, broken into small pieces

Preheat oven to 350° F. Butter a large loaf pan. Line bottom with a rectangle of wax paper. Butter the paper and sprinkle with flour. Shake out excess flour.

Put dates and raisins into a mixing bowl. Dissolve baking soda with boiling water and pour it over the date mixture.

Cream together the sugar and ½ cup butter. Beat in vanilla and egg. Add flour and mix well. Add date mixture including the liquid, then walnuts.

Pour mixture into pan, place in oven and bake for 1 hour, or until the top of the cake is dark brown and a knife inserted in the center comes out clean. Let cool about 5 minutes and unmold onto a rack. Remove the paper and let cool completely.

# LEMON BREAD

*Easy to make, this sweet tea bread has a nice tang from the lemon and yogurt.*

| | |
|---|---|
| 3 | cups flour |
| 1 | teaspoon baking soda |
| 1 | teaspoon salt |
| ½ | teaspoon baking powder |
| 3 | eggs |
| 1¾ | cups sugar |
| 1 | cup vegetable oil |
| 16 | ounces plain yogurt |
| 1 | tablespoon freshly grated lemon peel |
| 1 | tablespoon fresh lemon juice |

Preheat oven to 325° F. Measure flour, baking soda, salt and baking powder into sifter. Sift into medium size bowl and set aside.

In large mixing bowl beat eggs until foamy. Add sugar and oil and beat for one minute. Add yogurt, grated lemon peel (avoid white pith) and lemon juice and beat until thoroughly blended. Add flour mixture and beat until smooth.

Pour batter into 2 greased and floured 9 x 5 x 3-inch loaf pans. Smooth batter and bake for 45 minutes to 1 hour or until bread is golden.

Cool on rack for 15 minutes then remove from pan to cool completely.

# PUMPKIN BREAD

MAKES 2 LARGE OR 4 SMALL LOAVES

| | |
|---|---|
| 3 | cups flour |
| 2½ | cups sugar |
| 2 | teaspoons baking soda |
| ½ | teaspoon baking powder |
| ¼ | teaspoon salt |
| 2 | teaspoons ground cloves |
| 1 | teaspoon cinnamon |
| 4 | eggs |
| 1 | cup water |
| 1 | cup oil |
| 1 | cup pumpkin |

Preheat oven to 350° F. Mix together flour, sugar, baking soda, baking powder, salt, cloves and cinnamon in large bowl. Beat together eggs, water, oil and pumpkin. Add to dry mixture. Mix well with wire whisk or large spoon.

Bake in 2 greased 9 x 5-inch loaf pans 45 to 50 minutes, or in 4 greased 5 x 3-inch loaves for 40 to 45 minutes. Bake until toothpick inserted in center of bread comes out clean.

Cool bread on wire rack 5 to 10 minutes before removing from pans.

# BLUEBERRY CRUMB CAKE

SERVES 12

*Rave reviews at the breakfast table.*

2¼ cups flour, divided

1 cup sugar

¾ cup (1½ sticks) unsalted butter, cut into small pieces

1 teaspoon baking soda

1 egg

½ cup plain low-fat yogurt

1 pint blueberries (2½ cups), divided

**LEMON GLAZE**

1½ cups unsifted confectioners' sugar

2 to 3 tablespoons lemon juice

Preheat oven to 375° F. Butter a round 10 x 1½-inch baking dish or a 10-inch springform pan.

In a large bowl, combine 2 cups of flour with the sugar. Using your fingers, rub in the butter until the mixture resembles coarse meal. Set 1½ cups of the mixture aside for the crumb topping.

In a small bowl, combine the remaining ¼ cup flour with baking soda and mix well. Add to the mealy mixture in the large bowl and mix well.

In another bowl, lightly beat the egg. Stir in the yogurt. Add to dry ingredients in large bowl and stir briefly until blended. Fold in 1 cup of the blueberries.

Spread the batter in the prepared dish and scatter the remaining 1½ cups blueberries on top. Sprinkle the reserved crumb mixture over the blueberries.

Set the dish on a cookie sheet and bake in the middle of the oven for 50 to 60 minutes or until the crumbs are golden and a tester inserted in the center of the cake comes out clean. Serve warm or at room temperature dusted with confectioners' sugar or drizzled with lemon glaze.

**TO MAKE LEMON GLAZE,** stir together confectioners' sugar and lemon juice until smooth (it will be thick). Drizzle in a cross-hatch pattern over top of cake.

# APRICOT-ALMOND COFFEE CAKE

SERVES 8

*Good for brunch or Sunday breakfast. This crunchy coffee cake can be put together in minutes.*

1½ cups flour

¾ cup sugar

2 teaspoons baking powder

½ teaspoon salt

½ cup chopped dried apricots, dates or prunes

½ cup ground almonds

1 egg

¾ cup milk

¼ cup vegetable oil

## COCONUT TOPPING

2 tablespoons flour

⅓ cup firmly packed brown sugar

½ teaspoon ground cinnamon

2 tablespoons butter, melted

½ cup flaked coconut

Preheat oven to 400° F. In a large bowl stir together flour, sugar, baking powder, salt, dried fruit and almonds.

In a medium bowl beat egg with milk and vegetable oil. Add to dry mixture, stirring until smooth. Batter will be fairly stiff. Spread batter in greased 8-inch square pan.

**To make coconut topping,** stir together flour, brown sugar and cinnamon in a small bowl. Add butter and blend. Stir in coconut. Sprinkle evenly over batter.

Bake 25 to 30 minutes until golden brown. Cool on rack for 10 minutes. Cut in squares and serve warm or at room temperature.

# BUTTERMILK WAFFLES OR PANCAKES

(a favorite from the original *Artist in the Kitchen*)

SERVES 6 TO 8

*This is it, the perfect waffle recipe. Leftover batter may be stored, covered, in refrigerator up to 2 days and used for pancakes or more waffles!*

2   cups sifted flour

3   teaspoons baking powder

1   teaspoon baking soda

1   teaspoon salt

2   cups buttermilk

4   eggs, well beaten

1   cup (2 sticks) butter or margarine, melted (or ¾ cup vegetable oil)

Sift dry ingredients, or stir well with a wire whisk. Mix buttermilk and eggs. Add to dry ingredients and stir or beat until smooth. Stir in melted butter or oil.

Cook in heated waffle iron or on pancake griddle.

# BLUEBERRY BUTTERMILK PANCAKES

SERVES 6 TO 8

*Similar but not the same, these delightful pancakes are a year-round favorite.*

2   cups sifted cake flour

4   teaspoons baking powder

½   teaspoon salt

4   eggs, separated

2   cups buttermilk

½   teaspoon cream of tartar

4   tablespoons (½ stick) unsalted butter, melted and cooled

2   cups fresh or frozen blueberries

*Butter for greasing griddle or skillet*

In a large bowl, combine the flour, baking powder and salt and whisk to blend. Set aside.

In a small bowl, gently beat the egg yolks and buttermilk to blend. In another bowl, beat the egg whites until foamy. Add the cream of tartar and continue beating until stiff peaks form. Set aside.

Add the yolk mixture to the flour mixture and mix lightly with a fork only until flour is moistened. Stir in butter. Batter should be lumpy; do not overmix. Gently fold in the beaten egg whites.

Preheat griddle or skillet. Lightly butter or oil the hot griddle before each batch of pancakes. Pour out the batter to make four-inch rounds. Quickly drop about 6 to 8 berries onto each pancake.

When golden brown, turn over and cook about 30 seconds on the other side.

# CHEESY CORNBREAD

SERVES 8

*This is a terrifically moist, buttery and chewy cornbread that will not dry out.*
*Cut in small squares or diamonds.*

| | |
|---|---|
| 1 | cup (2 sticks) butter |
| ½ | cup sugar |
| 4 | eggs |
| 1½ | cups fresh, canned or frozen corn |
| ½ | cup Monterey Jack cheese, shredded |
| ½ | cup Cheddar cheese, shredded |
| 1 | cup flour |
| 1 | cup yellow corn meal |
| 2 | teaspoons baking powder |
| 1 | teaspoon salt |

Preheat oven to 325° F. Cream butter and sugar. Add eggs slowly, one at a time. Add remaining ingredients and mix until well incorporated.

Pour into a buttered 9-inch square pan. Bake for approximately one hour.

# FOCACCIA WITH ONIONS

SERVES 6 TO 10

## DOUGH

2   tablespoons dry yeast (or 2 packages)

1   cup plus 2 tablespoons lukewarm water

2   cups unbleached flour

1½ cups whole wheat flour

½   teaspoon salt

1   teaspoon sugar

2   tablespoons olive oil, plus about
    2 tablespoons more for oiling bowl,
    baking sheet and dough

Cornmeal

## ONION-HERB TOPPING

¼   cup olive oil

4   medium onions, peeled and sliced thin
    (2 cups)

1   teaspoon dried rosemary
    (or 2 teaspoons fresh)

¼   pound pancetta*, cut into thin strips

Coarse salt and freshly ground black pepper
to taste

Put the yeast, water, both flours, salt and sugar into the container of a food processor. Start blending while adding 2 tablespoons olive oil. Blend until dough comes away from the side of the container. Turn dough out onto a lightly floured board and knead briefly. Shape dough into a ball and put into a lightly oiled mixing bowl. Cover with plastic wrap and let rise in a warm place for an hour or more.

**TO PREPARE TOPPING,** heat the olive oil in a skillet and add onions, rosemary and pancetta. Cook very slowly over low heat, stirring occasionally, until the onions are golden brown and the pancetta cooked (about 15 to 20 minutes). Set aside.

Preheat oven to 400° F. (baking stone also if one is to be used). Lightly oil a baking sheet and sprinkle generously with cornmeal. Roll out or press the dough flat into a rectangle about ½-inch thick. Rub the surface with a tablespoon of olive oil. Make fingertip indentions over the surface leaving about a half-inch border all around. Spread the onion mixture evenly over the dough and press in lightly. Then press in grains of coarse salt and freshly ground pepper, if desired.

Slide the focaccia onto the baking stone (or leave on the baking sheet). Bake for 20 to 25 minutes until browned. Cut into squares and serve warm or at room temperature.

* Available in specialty food stores, or crisply browned bacon or Canadian bacon can be substituted.

# Homemade Pizza

¾ cup lukewarm water, divided

2 teaspoons dry yeast (or 1 package)

¼ cup rye flour

1 tablespoon milk

5 tablespoons olive oil, divided

½ teaspoon salt, or to taste

1¾ cups unbleached flour, plus more
for kneading

## TOPPING

2 medium yellow onions, halved and
thinly sliced

2 large tomatoes, peeled, seeded and diced

3 ounces Chevre, Feta or Monterey Jack
cheese, crumbled

1 tablespoon chopped, fresh Italian parsley

Pepperoni or cooked Italian sausage,
crumbled (optional)

In a mixing bowl, combine ¼ cup lukewarm water, yeast and rye flour. Blend well and cover with a towel. Let stand in a warm place for 20 to 30 minutes.

Add remaining ½ cup warm water, milk, 2 tablespoons olive oil, salt and flour. Mix dough with a wooden spoon, then knead it on a lightly floured board. It will be soft and a bit sticky. Add a little more flour to the board as you knead, but do not add any more flour than absolutely necessary. Knead for about 10 minutes.

Lightly oil inside of a mixing bowl and place dough in it. Turn the dough to lightly oil the top. Cover with a towel and let the dough rise in a warm place for about 2 hours, or until doubled in bulk. Punch it down, shape it, return to bowl and cover. Let rise 40 minutes longer.

Put pizza pan on a rack in oven and preheat oven to 500° F. Flatten dough on a floured board and roll it into a round about ⅛ to ¼-inch thick. Flour a wooden paddle or baking sheet and transfer the dough to it.

TO PREPARE THE TOPPING, heat 1 tablespoon of olive oil in a skillet and cook the onions until they are wilted. Scatter the onions over the dough. Sprinkle with diced tomatoes, soft crumbled cheese, parsley and pepperoni or sausage, if desired. Drizzle 2 tablespoons of olive oil over the top.

Slide the dough from the paddle onto the pizza pan. Bake 12 to 15 minutes until golden brown and crisp.

# No-Knead Baguettes

*A prize well within reach for the novice bread baker.*

3 cups lukewarm water

1 tablespoon dry yeast (or 1 package)

1 tablespoon sugar

6 to 7 cups unbleached all-purpose flour

2 teaspoons salt

1 egg white beaten with 1 tablespoon water
for glaze

In a large (4-quart) bowl, dissolve the yeast and sugar in the warm water. Let stand for about 10 minutes until bubbly. Add the salt and 6 cups of flour and mix thoroughly. Do not knead. The dough should be stiff; add up to 1 more cup of flour if the dough is too moist. Cover bowl with plastic wrap and allow dough to rise in a warm place for several hours, until it has doubled or tripled in bulk.

Turn the dough out onto a well-floured board. It will be sticky. Divide into 4 pieces with a sharp knife and let it rest for a few minutes.

Grease 2 double baguette pans. Shape each quarter of dough into a long loaf a little shorter than the pan and place in the pans. With a sharp knife, make 3 or 4 slashes, about ¼-inch deep, on the top of each loaf and cover lightly with a towel. (Free-form loaves can be baked on a cookie sheet if baguette pans are not available.)

Preheat oven to 425° F. and put a pan of hot water on the floor of oven or on lowest rack. When the dough has doubled in bulk, lightly brush the tops of the loaves with the glaze.

Bake for 10 minutes, brush with the glaze once more, and continue baking for another 10 to 15 minutes. Loaves should be crusty and brown when done.

Cool on a wire rack. Best eaten the same day, but can be wrapped in foil and frozen up to 6 weeks.

**Note:** *Substitute whole wheat flour, wheat germ, corn meal, etc. for part of the white flour to achieve taste and texture that appeal to you.*

# YOGURT BREAD (a favorite from the original *Artist in the Kitchen*)

MAKES 2 LOAVES

1   tablespoon dry yeast

2   cups warm water (105 to 115° F.)

2   tablespoons honey

1   cup plain yogurt

2   teaspoons salt

1½ cups rye flour

3   cups whole wheat flour

2 to 3 cups unbleached flour

Preheat oven to 350° F. Combine yeast, water and honey and let stand about 10 minutes to proof.

Stir in yogurt, salt, rye and whole wheat flours. Add unbleached flour gradually to make a dough that can be turned out on a floured board and kneaded. Knead about 10 minutes. Add more flour as needed to make a smooth, elastic dough (which is always a bit sticky).

Divide dough, form 2 loaves, and put in well-greased bread pans. Cover and let rise until dough rises just above rims. Bake about 45 minutes. Turn out and cool on rack.

**Note:**  *This fairly dense bread has a nice chewy texture, especially when toasted. It is easy and quick to make because it rises only once – in the pans.*

# WHOLE WHEAT ENGLISH MUFFINS

MAKES ABOUT 28 MUFFINS

2  tablespoons dry yeast (or 2 packages)

2  teaspoons sugar

3  cups lukewarm water

¾  cup dry milk

½  cup canola (or other vegetable) oil

⅓  cup honey

2  teaspoons salt

2½ cups whole wheat flour

½  cup wheat germ

3 to 4 cups unbleached flour

Cornmeal

In large bowl of an electric mixer dissolve yeast and sugar in water. Add dry milk. Let stand for 10 to 15 minutes until foamy.

Add oil, honey, salt, whole wheat flour and wheat germ. Beat at medium speed for 2 minutes (or 200 strokes by hand). Stir in enough unbleached flour to make a soft dough. (Amount varies according to heat and humidity.)

Turn out on a floured board and knead – adding more flour as necessary – until dough is smooth and elastic. Clean and oil bowl. Place dough in bowl, turning to coat all sides. Cover and let rise until doubled.

Sprinkle two cookie sheets generously with cornmeal. Punch down dough and turn out on a lightly floured board. Roll out about ½-inch thick. Cut into rounds with a 3-inch cutter (or a clean tuna can with both ends removed). Place rounds on cookie sheets and dust with more cornmeal. Cover and let rise until almost doubled.

Preheat a griddle to medium high (or an electric skillet to 325° F.). Do not grease the cooking surface. Cook muffins about 8 to 12 minutes on each side or until evenly browned. Cool to room temperature on racks. Use forks to split muffins and toast before serving.

# SALADS

*Detail from the fabric "Pomegranate"*

*produced by William Morris and Company*

*in England during the turn of this century.*

# INSALATA CHECCA*

SERVES 4 TO 6

*This perfect summer salad presents a wonderful contrast of golden garlicky croutons with juicy ripe tomatoes.*

4    large ripe tomatoes, chopped

3    cloves garlic, minced

2    tablespoons chopped fresh parsley

1    tablespoon chopped fresh basil

1½ cups olive oil, divided

Salt and freshly ground pepper to taste

2    sprigs fresh rosemary

3    cups day-old Italian or sourdough bread, cut into ½-inch cubes

Fresh basil leaves

Mix tomatoes (do not discard seeds or liquid), garlic, parsley, basil and ½ cup olive oil in a bowl. Season with salt and pepper. Refrigerate for 2 hours.

Heat remaining olive oil in a skillet. When it is very hot but not smoking, sauté the rosemary and bread until it is golden brown. Lift bread out of pan with a slotted spoon and place on a paper towel to drain and cool.

When ready to serve, place bread cubes on pretty glass plate or bowl and top with tomato mixture, including enough juice to moisten the bread. Garnish with whole basil leaves.

* From Pane Caldo Restaurant, Los Angeles, California

# SNOW PEA SALAD

SERVES 4 TO 6

*A winsome winter salad you can assemble in minutes.*

12 to 16 ounces snow peas, trimmed and stringed

1    bunch scallions, chopped

⅓   cup vegetable oil

1    tablespoon fresh lemon juice

1    tablespoon white wine vinegar

½   teaspoon salt

½   teaspoon sugar

1    clove garlic, minced

1    cup cherry tomatoes, halved

1    (5-ounce) can water chestnuts, drained and sliced

Blanch snow peas in boiling water for 30 seconds. Drain and chill.

Whisk together vegetable oil, lemon juice, vinegar, salt, sugar and garlic. Just before serving pour over snow peas and toss gently with scallions, tomatoes and water chestnuts.

# ROASTED PEPPER SALAD

SERVES 6

*Serve this as a first course or a light lunch with fresh Mozzarella.*

1   large ripe summer tomato

1   clove garlic, minced

5    fresh basil leaves, torn into thirds

15  whole fresh mint leaves, divided

¼   cup olive oil

4   red or yellow bell peppers,
     or combination

2   tablespoons capers in wine
     vinegar, drained

Dice the tomato and place in a glass bowl. Add garlic, basil and 5 of the mint leaves. Pour oil over the top and refrigerate for 1 hour.

Prepare roasted red and yellow peppers according to instructions on page 75. Cut the peeled peppers into thin strips. Pour tomato mixture over them.

Mix well, cover and refrigerate for at least 1 hour. To serve, sprinkle the remaining mint leaves and capers over the peppers.

# RED ONION AND BLACK OLIVE SALAD

SERVES 4

4   red onions, thinly sliced

1   cup finely chopped imported black olives
     (Kalamata or Italian)

½   cup vegetable oil

2   tablespoons soy sauce

1   tablespoon dry sherry

1   tablespoon vinegar

½   teaspoon freshly ground black pepper

2   tablespoons finely chopped fresh parsley

¼   pound crumbled Roquefort cheese

Put onion slices in a bowl and cover with ice water for 1 hour until crisp. Drain. Pat dry with paper towels. Return to bowl and sprinkle with black olives.

Combine oil, soy sauce, sherry, vinegar and pepper. Pour over onions, sprinkle with parsley and cheese. Refrigerate for several hours before serving.

# SOUTHWESTERN SALAD VINAIGRETTE

*Serve this fiesta salad in a clear glass bowl or for bolder contrast in a black speckled earthenware dish. Teams up well with any grilled meat or fish.*

| | |
|---|---|
| 2 | cups canned black beans, rinsed and drained |
| 2 | red bell peppers, seeded and cut into ¾-inch pieces |
| 2 | green bell peppers, seeded and cut into ¾-inch pieces |
| 2 | cups corn kernels (fresh or frozen, defrosted) |
| 1 | tablespoon cumin seeds |
| ¼ | cup sherry wine vinegar |
| 1 | tablespoon Dijon mustard |
| 2 | teaspoons salt |
| 2 | teaspoons freshly ground black pepper |
| ¼ | cup canola oil |
| ¼ | cup olive oil |
| 18 | cherry tomatoes, cut in half |
| 3 | scallions, thinly sliced |

In a large bowl, combine beans, peppers and corn. In small dry skillet, toast cumin seeds over moderately high heat, tossing, until golden brown, about 1 minute. Grind in spice mill or finely chop on cutting board.

In a food processor or bowl, whisk together vinegar, mustard, cumin seeds, salt and pepper. Slowly whisk in oil. Pour dressing over salad and toss well.

Add tomatoes and scallions to salad, toss and season with additional salt and pepper to taste. Serve at room temperature.

**Note:** *Can be made 1 day ahead; bring to room temperature and add tomatoes and scallions just before serving.*

56

# TOMATOES WITH ARMAGNAC

SERVES 4

*A modest amount of this bracing and aromatic brandy yields a lush tomato.*

1   pound ripe summer tomatoes

Sugar to taste (optional)

Salt and freshly ground pepper to taste

1   teaspoon Armagnac (fruity, robust
    brandy from southwestern France)

2½ tablespoons walnut oil

1   teaspoon sherry wine vinegar

2   teaspoons minced shallots

2   teaspoons minced fresh parsley

Cut tomatoes in half horizontally. Gently squeeze out juice and remove seeds. Cut into slices. Spread out on a plate. Sprinkle with sugar, salt, pepper and Armagnac. Let stand for 2 to 3 hours. Drain.

Whisk together oil and vinegar and drizzle over the tomatoes. Sprinkle shallots and parsley on top.

# ARTICHOKE AND ARUGULA SALAD

SERVES 4 TO 6

*This fresh, crisp salad with beautiful colors is substantial.*

3   (5-ounce) jars marinated artichoke
    hearts, drained and sliced thin

1   small fennel bulb, cleaned and chopped
    medium fine

1   rib celery, chopped medium fine

3   tablespoons olive oil, divided

3   tablespoons balsamic vinegar, divided

1   bunch arugula (or watercress), washed,
    dried and torn into bite-sized pieces

1   small head radicchio, washed, dried
    and torn into bite-sized pieces

¼   pound freshly grated Parmesan or
    Asiago cheese, divided

Salt and freshly ground pepper to taste

In medium-sized bowl, mix artichoke hearts with fennel, celery, 1 tablespoon olive oil and 1 tablespoon vinegar. Add arugula, radicchio, most of the cheese and remaining olive oil and vinegar. Season with salt and pepper and toss thoroughly. Sprinkle remaining cheese on top.

# APPLE SALAD WITH BLUE CHEESE

SERVES 4

*A satiny spirited dressing embraces crunchy apples, tarted up with peppery greens.*

| | |
|---|---|
| 3 | tablespoons fresh lemon juice |
| ¼ | teaspoon salt |
| ½ | cup corn oil |
| 1 | tablespoon honey |
| 2 to 3 | tablespoons Calvados (or other apple brandy) |
| 2 | crisp, tart apples, peeled, cored and diced |
| 2 | ribs celery, diced |
| ½ | cup walnuts, coarsely chopped |
| 1 | large bunch arugula (or watercress), washed, dried and torn into bite-sized pieces |
| ½ | cup crumbled blue cheese |

Combine lemon juice and salt in a blender or food processor. With the motor running on low speed, add in the oil in a slow, steady stream. Fold in the honey and Calvados to taste.

Place apples and celery in bowl with walnuts. Spoon enough dressing over the mixture to coat.

Arrange arugula in a shallow salad bowl. Spoon the apple mixture into the center. Sprinkle the cheese around the edge. Serve with the remaining dressing on the side.

# HUNTER'S SALAD (a favorite from the original *Artist in the Kitchen*)

SERVES 4

| | |
|---|---|
| ⅓ | cup vinegar |
| 1 | cup vegetable oil |
| ¼ | cup sugar |
| ¼ | cup grated onion |
| 1 | teaspoon dry mustard |
| 1 | teaspoon salt |
| 1 | teaspoon celery seed |
| 1 | pound spinach leaves, well-washed and dried |
| 1 | small red onion, thinly sliced |
| 2 | firm red apples |
| 4 | tablespoons toasted almonds, walnuts or pine nuts |

Put first seven ingredients into blender or food processor and blend 6 seconds. Toss dressing with spinach leaves and top with onion rings, thinly sliced unpeeled apples and toasted nuts.

# MOROCCAN-STYLE BEET SALAD

SERVES 4

*Worth staining your fingers for, this is one of our favorite salads.*

1   pound fresh beets

1   teaspoon sugar

Juice of 1 lemon

1   tablespoon olive oil

¼   teaspoon cinnamon

1   tablespoon chopped fresh parsley

Salt to taste

Wash beets. Cut off tops, leaving about one inch. Boil, covered, until tender. Cool, slip off the skins, trim off the tops and cut into bite-sized cubes.

Mix the remaining ingredients, pour over the beets and toss gently. Let sit one 1 hour before serving.

# MARRAKESH SPINACH SALAD

SERVES 4

*A wilted spinach salad with a spicy dressing.*

4   cups fresh spinach or a combination
    of spinach, watercress and/or arugula,
    tightly packed

1   cup parsley sprigs, tightly packed

½   cup fresh cilantro, tightly packed

1 to 2 large cloves garlic, peeled

Salt to taste

3   tablespoons olive oil

½   cup imported black olives
    (Kalamata or Italian), pitted

¼   teaspoon paprika

Cayenne to taste

Fresh lemon juice to taste

Wash the spinach and other greens and cut off stems. Cook, covered, in ½ cup water until just wilted. Drain and chop. When cool enough to handle, squeeze out as much moisture as possible. Set aside.

Wash and dry the parsley and cilantro. Place herbs and garlic in bowl of food processor and process until very fine, almost to a paste. Add ¼ teaspoon salt. Chop very fine, almost to a paste (or grind them to a paste with a mortar and pestle).

Heat oil in a skillet and add herb paste. Cook 2 to 3 minutes over medium heat. Add spinach and greens and sauté for about 3 minutes or until any liquid has evaporated. Stir in olives, salt, paprika and cayenne to taste. Cool.

Just before serving sprinkle with lemon juice. Serve chilled.

**Note:** *This salad will keep, covered, in the refrigerator for several days.*

# WILD RICE AND TABOULLEH

SERVES 8 TO 10

*A great side dish for a summer dinner or a light lunch entree.*

¾   cup Taboulleh mix*

2   cups chicken broth
    (homemade or canned)

¾   cup wild rice, rinsed and drained

3   medium tomatoes, diced

1   cup chopped fresh parsley

¼   cup finely chopped scallions

¼   cup fresh lemon juice

2   cloves garlic, minced

½   teaspoon salt

¼   cup olive oil

*Freshly ground pepper to taste*

Soak taboulleh and accompanying spices in 6 cups hot water for 1 hour. Drain well. Bring chicken broth to a boil, add rice and simmer for 50 to 60 minutes, until rice is tender but crunchy and most of the liquid is absorbed. Drain if necessary. Let cool.

In salad bowl, combine bulgur, rice, tomatoes, parsley and scallions. Combine lemon juice, garlic and salt; blend well. Add oil and whisk until mixed. Season with pepper.

Pour over salad, toss gently. Cover and refrigerate until serving time or for up to 2 days.

* Found in rice section of most supermarkets.

# SESAME CHICKEN SALAD

SERVES 6

3   pounds skinless, boneless chicken breasts,
    rinsed and patted dry

⅓   cup plus 3 teaspoons Oriental sesame oil

½   teaspoon cayenne (or more to taste)

1   teaspoon wine vinegar

1½  tablespoons soy sauce

1½  tablespoons honey

⅛   teaspoon allspice

¼   cup vegetable oil

½   pound snow peas, trimmed and stringed

¾   cup pecan halves, toasted lightly

¼   cup toasted sesame seeds

½   cup thinly sliced scallions

Preheat oven to 350° F. Cut chicken into 1-inch cubes. Arrange in a single layer on a flat pan. Drizzle with ⅓ cup of the sesame oil and sprinkle on cayenne. Bake for 8 to 10 minutes. Remove chicken from the pan and set aside.

In a large bowl whisk together the vinegar, soy sauce, honey, allspice and a pinch more cayenne if desired. Add the vegetable oil and the remaining sesame oil.

Blanch the snow peas for 5 seconds in boiling water. Drain, refresh them under cold water and pat dry.

Toss the chicken with the dressing and let it stand for 1 hour. Just before serving add the snow peas, pecans, sesame seeds, scallions, salt and pepper to taste.

# CHICKEN CAESAR SALAD

SERVES 4

*Can be prepared with leftover grilled chicken as well.*

## CHICKEN

4   skinless, boneless chicken breasts, rinsed and patted dry

2   tablespoons olive oil

1   tablespoon fresh parsley, chopped

1   clove garlic, minced

Salt and freshly ground pepper to taste

## CROUTONS

1   tablespoon olive oil

1   small garlic clove, minced

2   cups day-old Italian bread cubes cut in ½-inch squares

## VINAIGRETTE

3   anchovy fillets, drained, patted dry (or 2 teaspoons anchovy paste)

1   clove garlic, minced

2   tablespoons fresh lemon juice

1   tablespoon red wine vinegar

½   cup olive oil

Salt and freshly ground pepper to taste

## SALAD

1   large head romaine lettuce, washed, dried and torn into bite-sized pieces

4   tablespoons freshly grated Parmesan or Romano cheese, divided

12   cherry tomatoes

1   avocado (optional)

**TO PREPARE CHICKEN,** combine olive oil, parsley, garlic, salt and pepper and rub onto both sides of chicken. Cover and refrigerate at least 1 hour.

**TO PREPARE CROUTONS,** combine olive oil and garlic in small bowl. Add bread cubes and toss to coat. Spread on baking sheet and bake in a preheated 350° F. oven until lightly toasted, tossing once, about 15 minutes. Set aside.

**TO PREPARE VINAIGRETTE,** purée anchovies (or anchovy paste) and garlic with lemon juice and vinegar in blender or food processor. With machine running, add oil in thin steady stream. Blend until smooth and emulsified. Season with salt and pepper and set aside.

When chicken is ready, remove from refrigerator and grill about 5 to 7 minutes per side or bake for about 25 minutes in a 350° F. oven. Cut into ¼-inch wide strips.

Toss lettuce with half the dressing, croutons and 2 tablespoons cheese. Divide mixture between 4 large plates and arrange chicken on top of lettuce. Garnish with tomatoes, remaining cheese and slices of avocado. Pass additional dressing.

# ORIENTAL SHRIMP SALAD

*East meets West. Subtle fresh ingredients deftly paired with a fragrant vinaigrette.*

## VINAIGRETTE

1   clove garlic, minced

1   teaspoon Dijon mustard

1   tablespoon balsamic vinegar

1½  tablespoons dark soy sauce

1   cup peanut oil

¼   cup Oriental sesame oil

## SHRIMP

1   clove garlic, minced

⅓   ounce fresh ginger, peeled and minced

8   scallions, chopped

¼   cup peanut oil

2   pounds shrimp, peeled, deveined, rinsed and patted dry

½   pound mushrooms, thinly sliced

2   heads Bibb lettuce, washed and dried

**TO PREPARE VINAIGRETTE,** combine garlic, mustard, vinegar, soy sauce, peanut oil and sesame oil in a food processor or large bowl and blend. Set aside.

Sauté garlic, ginger, scallions and shrimp in ¼ cup peanut oil over medium high heat until just cooked. Drain and combine with vinaigrette.

Toss and serve at room temperature or slightly chilled over a bed of mushrooms and lettuce.

62

# ROAST BEEF SALAD

SERVES 6

*Last night's beef becomes today's lunch. Have plenty of good French bread and a crock of sweet butter on hand.*

## VINAIGRETTE

¼   cup wine vinegar or fresh lemon juice

2   tablespoons Dijon mustard

1   teaspoon salt

*Freshly ground pepper to taste*

1   cup olive oil

## SALAD

1   pound green beans

2   pounds red potatoes

¼   cup minced shallots

3   tablespoons beef broth
    (homemade or canned)

2   pounds cooked (rare) roast beef,
    sirloin steak, flank steak, or beef
    tenderloin, sliced ¼-inch thick
    and cut into strips

2   red onions, thinly sliced

*Snipped fresh chives*

*Chopped fresh parsley*

In a small bowl whisk together vinegar, mustard, salt and pepper. Gradually whisk in olive oil. Set vinaigrette aside.

Cook the green beans in boiling salted water to cover for 7 to 8 minutes until just crisp-tender. Drain, rinse with cold water and a dry. Cut into uniform lengths and toss with ½ cup of the vinaigrette.

Boil the potatoes until easily pierced with a sharp knife. Peel, thinly slice and combine while still warm with minced shallots and beef broth. Toss until the broth is absorbed. Add the remaining vinaigrette and toss to coat the potatoes well.

In a large salad bowl arrange the green beans, potato slices, and roast beef and decorate with onion rings. Sprinkle the salad with chives and parsley. Serve at room temperature.

63

*Salads*

# ITALIAN FENNEL BEAN SALAD

*A great luncheon alternative to the traditional Niçoise, particularly in winter.*

| | |
|---|---|
| 1 | medium fennel bulb, thinly sliced |
| ½ | medium red onion, thinly sliced |
| 1 | (15-ounce) can cannellini or navy beans, rinsed and drained |
| 1 | (6⅛-ounce) can tuna fish, drained |
| 6 | tablespoons olive oil |
| 2 | tablespoons wine vinegar or fresh lemon juice |
| 1 | teaspoon Dijon mustard |
| 1 | clove garlic, minced |

Salt and freshly ground pepper to taste

Lettuce

Imported black olives (Kalamata or Italian)

Tomato wedges

Sliced hard-boiled eggs

In a large bowl, mix together fennel, onion, beans, and tuna. Set aside.

In a small bowl whisk together olive oil, vinegar, mustard, garlic, salt and pepper. Gently toss vegetables and tuna with vinaigrette.

To serve, spoon onto lettuce leaves and garnish with olives, tomatoes and hard-boiled eggs. Serve with pita bread or bagel chips.

# SUMMER CARROT SLAW

*This untraditional slaw looks beautiful on a plate and goes with everything.*

| | |
|---|---|
| 6 | medium carrots, peeled |
| ¼ | cup olive oil |
| ½ | teaspoon dry mustard |
| ½ | teaspoon dried basil |
| 1 | clove garlic, minced |
| 1 | tablespoon chopped scallion tops |
| 1 | tablespoon pickle relish |
| 1 | tablespoon fresh lemon juice |
| 1½ | tablespoons vinegar |

Shred carrots in food processor. Set aside. Combine remaining ingredients. Pour over carrots.

Cover and refrigerate for at least 1 hour or overnight. Serve chilled. Keeps refrigerated for a week.

# CITRUS VINAIGRETTE

MAKES 1 CUP

*A tangy alternative for salads that contain grapefruit, oranges and/or avocado.*

3   tablespoons white wine vinegar

3   tablespoons fresh orange juice

1½ tablespoons fresh grapefruit juice

1½ tablespoons Dijon mustard

1   teaspoon salt

1½ tablespoons sugar

½   cup vegetable oil

2   tablespoons poppy seeds (optional)

Combine all ingredients except the oil and the optional poppy seeds in a blender, food processor or jar until well mixed. Add the oil and blend well. Refrigerate. Shake well before using.

# CREAMY DRESSING FOR LEAFY GREENS OR CUCUMBERS (a favorite from the original *Artist in the Kitchen*)

MAKES ABOUT 1¼ CUPS

1   cup sour cream

2   tablespoons fresh lemon juice

1   tablespoon grated onion

*Freshly ground pepper to taste*

1   teaspoon Worcestershire sauce

¼   teaspoon salt

1   teaspoon sugar

*Finely minced fresh parsley*

Combine sour cream with remaining ingredients in blender or food processor. Blend until smooth. Chill 30 minutes.

Serve on salad greens or chilled cucumbers with thinly sliced mild onion. Garnish with minced parsley.

# Basil Oil

1    cup tightly packed fresh basil leaves

2    cups olive oil

In a large pan of boiling salted water, blanch basil leaves for 5 seconds. Drain and rinse with cold water.

In food processor or blender, purée blanched basil with ¼ cup of oil. With the machine on, add the remaining 1¾ cups oil and process until well blended and smooth. Transfer to a glass jar, cover and let stand at room temperature for at least 24 hours.

Carefully pour off the clear green oil, leaving behind the basil purée which may be discarded. The strained oil can be refrigerated, covered, for up to 1 month.

**Note:** *You can also use this flavored oil tossed with pasta or rice or drizzled over tomatoes and poached fish or chicken.*

# Orange and Basil Vinaigrette

MAKES ½ CUP

Freshly grated peel of 1 orange

2    cups fresh orange juice

¼    cup basil oil (see previous recipe)

Salt and freshly ground pepper to taste

In a medium nonreactive saucepan, combine the peel and orange juice and bring to a boil over moderately high heat; boil until reduced to ¼ cup, about 20 minutes.

Strain the juice into a small bowl and let cool slightly. Stir in the basil oil and season with salt and pepper to taste. Use immediately or refrigerate the vinaigrette in a covered jar or bottle for up to 2 weeks. Let return to room temperature before serving.

# DIJON VINAIGRETTE

MAKES 1 CUP

*An excellent vinaigrette for tossed greens, French potato salad, cold green beans or cold asparagus.*

1    tablespoon Dijon mustard

4    tablespoons red wine vinegar

1    teaspoon sugar

½    teaspoon salt

½    teaspoon freshly ground black pepper

1    tablespoon freshly grated onion

3    tablespoons minced fresh parsley or snipped fresh chives

½    cup olive oil

Combine all ingredients except the oil in a blender, food processor or jar and process until well mixed. Add oil and blend well.

The vinaigrette is best if made just before using, but it can be refrigerated. Shake well before using.

# A VERY SIMPLE VINAIGRETTE

1    clove garlic, halved (optional)

Olive oil

Red wine vinegar

Dijon mustard (optional)

Salt and freshly ground pepper to taste

Crumbled cheese such as goat or Roquefort (optional)

Shortly before serving, rub a wooden salad bowl with a cut clove of garlic. Place washed and dried greens (no iceberg please) in bowl. Drizzle just enough oil over leaves to coat lightly when tossed. Lightly sprinkle vinegar over all (mixed with some Dijon mustard if desired), toss and taste. Add a bit more vinegar if necessary. Season with salt and pepper, add crumbled cheese, if desired, and serve immediately.

**Note:** *This dressing requires no measuring or mixing but a very light touch with the oil and vinegar. The point is to just coat the leaves until they glisten so the salad remains fresh and crisp, not soggy. If made properly, there should be no dressing found at the bottom of the bowl.*

# SOUPS

*Detail from a 15th century Spanish silk*

*fabric showing Moorish design influences.*

# CURRIED SUMMER SQUASH SOUP

SERVES 6

*This summer soup is delicious hot or cold. Serve plain or dress the soup up with the suggested garnishes for a more important presentation.*

1    cup chopped leeks or onions
     (if using leeks, wash well and use
     white part only)

2    tablespoons butter or vegetable oil

1    tablespoon curry powder

⅛    teaspoon red pepper flakes (optional)

¼    teaspoon black pepper

½    teaspoon salt

2    pounds yellow squash,
     scrubbed and chopped

2    cups chicken broth (homemade
     or canned)

Yogurt or sour cream, chives, toasted
coconut (optional garnishes)

In a heavy-bottomed saucepan, sauté leeks in butter until soft. Stir in curry powder, red pepper, pepper and salt and cook a few minutes.

Add squash and broth. Cover and simmer about 20 minutes until squash is tender. Purée small quantities at a time in a food processor or blender. Pour into bowls and garnish as desired. Serve hot or cold.

**Note:** *The red pepper flakes "light" the curry flavor and brighten this soup.*

# SPRING PEA SOUP

SERVES 6

*So easily prepared, this verdant purée sings spring.*

4    tablespoons (½ stick) unsalted butter

1    medium onion, coarsely chopped (½ cup)

2    large cloves garlic, minced

4    cups chicken broth (homemade
     or canned)

1    large Idaho potato, peeled and quartered

1½   pounds frozen sweet peas

¼    teaspoon cayenne pepper

½    teaspoon freshly ground black pepper

2    tablespoons dried tarragon

Melt the butter in a heavy saucepan over low heat. Add the onion and garlic, and cook gently until wilted, about 10 minutes.

Add the broth and potato; bring to a boil. Reduce heat and cook, covered, until potato is just tender, about 15 minutes.

Add peas, cayenne and black pepper, and return to a boil. Then remove pan from heat and stir in tarragon.

Allow to cool, uncovered, for 10 minutes. Process the soup, small quantities at a time, in a food processor or blender until smooth. Pour through a fine sieve or a food mill to remove any pieces of skin. Serve warm.

# FRENCH SPLIT PEA SOUP

SERVES 4 TO 5

*A surefire quickly prepared success. We love these foolproof recipes for big cauldrons of old-fashioned, down-to-earth soup.*

2  cups dried split green peas, rinsed and drained

6  cups chicken broth (homemade or canned), divided

¼  teaspoon dried thyme

3  tablespoons minced fresh parsley

4 or 5 ribs celery, with leaves, chopped

1  bay leaf

Ham bone (optional)

5  tablespoons butter, divided

½  cup chopped carrots

¾  cup chopped onions

1  cup chopped spinach or leaf lettuce

Salt and freshly ground pepper to taste

In a large soup pot put peas, 5 cups of broth, thyme, parsley, celery, bay leaf and ham bone. Simmer, covered, about 30 minutes until peas are tender.

Meanwhile in a large skillet melt 3 tablespoons butter and sauté carrots, onions and chopped spinach or lettuce until soft. Add the sautéed vegetables to the split peas and broth and simmer for 30 minutes.

Soup may be puréed, small quantities at a time, in a food processor or blender if a creamy texture is desired. Add reserved cup of broth if soup is too thick.

Season with salt and pepper. Stir in remaining butter just prior to serving. ✿

*71*

**Soups**

# HOT ZUCCHINI SOUP (a favorite from the original *Artist in the Kitchen*)

SERVES 6 TO 8

*Sticks to the ribs! This is a rousing concoction, good for a simple supper.*

1   pound Italian sweet sausage, crumbled

2   cups chopped celery

1   clove garlic, minced

2   pounds zucchini, scrubbed and chopped
    in ½-inch pieces

2   medium onions, chopped (1 cup)

2   (15-ounce) cans of tomatoes with liquid,
    or about 10 medium tomatoes, peeled

2   teaspoons salt

1   teaspoon dried oregano

1   teaspoon sugar

1   teaspoon dried basil

¼   teaspoon dried thyme

2   green bell peppers, cut in ½-inch pieces

Freshly grated Parmesan or Romano cheese

In a large, heavy-bottomed cooking pot brown sausage and drain fat. Add celery and garlic and cook over medium heat for about 10 minutes. Add other ingredients except green pepper and cheese.

Simmer, covered, for 20 minutes. Add green pepper and simmer, covered, 10 minutes longer.

Ladle into bowls and sprinkle with freshly grated cheese.

72

# FRESH MUSHROOM SOUP

SERVES 6

1  pound fresh mushrooms

4  cups chicken broth
   (homemade or canned)

1  medium onion, finely chopped (½ cup)

6  tablespoons (¾ stick) butter

6  tablespoons flour

3  cups milk

1  cup heavy cream

1  teaspoon salt

White pepper to taste

Tabasco sauce to taste

2  tablespoons sherry

Finely minced fresh parsley

Wash and dry mushrooms. Cut off stems and chop very fine. Simmer, covered, in broth with onion for 30 minutes. Melt butter in a saucepan, add flour and stir with wire whisk until blended.

Meanwhile in another pan, bring milk to a boil and add all at once to the butter/flour mixture, stirring vigorously with whisk until sauce is thickened and smooth. Add cream. Combine mushroom broth mixture with sauce and season to taste with salt, pepper and tabasco. Add sherry last. Garnish with parsley.

# PEANUT SOUP

SERVES 6 TO 8

*Exotic and aromatic, this soup is a front runner. The lime and ginger add nice tangy notes.*

⅓    cup vegetable oil

2    large onions, finely chopped (2 cups)

1    teaspoon minced garlic

1    teaspoon minced fresh ginger

1    tablespoon ground coriander

1    teaspoon freshly ground pepper

½    teaspoon turmeric

5    cups chicken broth (homemade or canned)

½    cup creamy peanut butter

1    tablespoon sesame paste (tahini)

3    tablespoons cornstarch dissolved in ¼ cup water

⅓    cup heavy cream

2    tablespoons fresh lime juice

Salt to taste

Chopped scallions

In a large saucepan, heat the oil. Add onions, garlic and ginger and cook over moderately high heat, stirring occasionally, until onions are lightly browned. Add coriander, pepper and turmeric and cook for 1 more minute.

Stir in chicken broth, peanut butter and sesame paste. Bring soup to a boil. Add cornstarch mixture and cook, stirring, until soup thickens, about 2 minutes. Stir in the cream and simmer over low heat until piping hot.

Add lime juice and salt. Serve hot, garnished with the scallions.

74

# RED PEPPER BISQUE

SERVES 6

3  large red bell peppers (about 2 pounds)

1  leek (white part only) well-washed and chopped

1  medium onion, chopped (½ cup)

2  tablespoons vegetable oil

1  tablespoon butter (optional)

3  tablespoons flour

2  cups hot chicken broth (homemade or canned)

2 to 2½ cups milk (depending on consistency desired)

Sprig of fresh thyme (or ½ teaspoon dried)

1  clove garlic, minced

½  teaspoon ground cloves

Salt and freshly ground pepper to taste

6  tablespoons sour cream

Fresh sprigs of rosemary, tarragon or thyme

TO ROAST RED PEPPERS, wash and pat peppers dry. Place on foil-covered baking pan. Broil under preheated broiler, 1½ to 2 inches from heat, turning every few minutes until skin blisters and chars.

Remove peppers to bowl and cover. When they are cool enough to handle, peel, cut off tops and discard seeds and ribs.

TO PREPARE PURÉE, blend in a food processor or blender and set aside. (Can be refrigerated for several days or frozen for later use.)

In a heavy bottomed saucepan cook leek and onion in oil and butter, covered, until soft and yellow. Stir in flour and cook for 3 minutes. Remove from heat and whisk in ½ cup of hot broth. Return to heat and stir until thickened. Stir in rest of broth, milk, thyme, garlic, cloves, salt and pepper.

Simmer, partly covered, 10 minutes. Add red pepper purée. Simmer 10 minutes more. Serve hot or chilled. Garnish each portion with 1 tablespoon sour cream and a sprig of fresh herb. ❀

# MINESTRONE SOUP

*Hearty fare for après winter sport, this rich vegetable soup is vibrant and full-bodied.*

1 pound dried small white pea beans, soaked overnight, rinsed and drained

3 tablespoons olive oil

3 medium onions, finely chopped (1½ cups)

3 leeks (white part only), well-washed and finely sliced

8 ribs celery, finely sliced

2 tablespoons tomato paste

¾ pound lean beef, cut in chunks

4 cloves garlic, minced

6 carrots, sliced

6 zucchini, sliced

6 ripe tomatoes, peeled and chopped or 1 (14½-ounce) can Italian plum tomatoes with juice

4 potatoes, diced

½ small cabbage, shredded

8 cups beef broth (homemade or canned)

Salt and freshly ground pepper to taste

1 (10-ounce) package tiny frozen peas

1 cup small pasta, such as macaroni

1 cup chopped fresh parsley or basil, alone or in combination

Freshly grated Parmesan cheese

Place beans in a large pot and cover with water. Cook slowly, uncovered, until tender, about 1½ hours.

Meanwhile, heat oil in heavy, large pot and sauté onions, leeks and celery until soft. Add tomato paste and beef and sauté 3 to 5 more minutes. Add garlic, carrots, zucchini, tomatoes, potatoes, cabbage, beef broth and salt and pepper to taste. Simmer uncovered until everything is just tender.

Add beans with some of their cooking liquid (to achieve desired consistency), peas, pasta, parsley and basil. Simmer until pasta is cooked but not too soft as it will continue to cook in hot soup.

Remove beef chunks, dice and return to soup. Correct seasoning. Ladle into bowls and pass freshly grated Parmesan cheese. ✿

# BLACK BEAN SOUP

*This gutsy soup is even better made at least a day in advance.*

½   pound smoked slab bacon with rind

3   medium onions, finely chopped
    (1½ cups)

1½ cups finely chopped celery

1½ cups finely diced carrots

1   bay leaf

1   tablespoon minced garlic

1¼ teaspoons dried thyme

4   tablespoons ground cumin, divided

1   teaspoon freshly ground black pepper

¼   cup finely chopped fresh oregano leaves
    (or 1 tablespoon dried)

3   tablespoons tomato paste

16  cups chicken broth, (homemade
    or canned)

1   pound dried black beans, soaked
    overnight, rinsed and drained
    (about 3 cups)

6   tablespoons fresh lime juice

¼   teaspoon cayenne pepper

Salt to taste

½   cup finely chopped fresh cilantro leaves

Salsa (see recipe page 30)

Sour cream

Slice off and reserve rind of the bacon. Cut bacon into ¼-inch cubes. There should be about 1½ cups. Put bacon cubes and rind into a heavy pot and cook, stirring often, until bacon cubes are crisp. Add onions, celery, carrots, bay leaf, garlic, thyme, 3 tablespoons of the cumin, black pepper and oregano. Stir to blend and cover.

Cook about 5 minutes over moderately low heat. Do not allow mixture to burn. Add tomato paste and stir briefly. Add chicken broth and bring to a boil. Add beans to the soup. Cook, uncovered, over relatively high heat about 2½ hours, skimming the surface occasionally to remove foam and fat as they rise to the top.

The soup is ready when the beans are soft and some of them have disintegrated. Stir in lime juice, cayenne pepper, salt, cilantro and remaining cumin.

Remove and discard the bacon rind and bay leaf. Ladle the soup into individual bowls and serve with salsa and sour cream if desired. ✸

**Note:** *This soup freezes very well.*

# WILD MUSHROOM SOUP

SERVES 6

1   tablespoon butter

1   large mild onion, such as Vidalia,
    chopped (1 cup)

1   clove garlic, minced

1   cup fresh wild mushrooms, such as
    oyster, shiitake, or hearty brown, alone
    or in combination, chopped

1   cup buttermilk

¾   cup sour cream (reserve ¼ cup
    for garnish)

1½  cups beef broth (homemade or canned)

2   tablespoons Madeira or dry sherry

1   cup water

¾   teaspoon salt

½   teaspoon freshly ground pepper

1   tablespoon cornstarch dissolved in ¼ cup
    lukewarm water

In a heavy-bottomed saucepan, melt butter and sauté onions and garlic for 2 minutes over medium heat. Do not brown.

Add mushrooms and cook, stirring frequently, for an additional 2 minutes. Remove from heat and cool slightly.

Purée mixture in blender or food processor. Return to saucepan, add remaining ingredients except for cornstarch and bring to a simmer. Whisk dissolved cornstarch into soup stirring constantly. Cook over medium heat for 3 to 5 minutes until thickened. Do not allow to boil.

Soup can be sieved if a velvety texture is desired. Ladle into serving bowls and serve with a dollop of reserved sour cream. ✹

# BUTTERNUT SOUP

SERVES 4 TO 6

1¼  pounds butternut or acorn squash

1   medium onion, chopped (½ cup)

½   cup sliced carrots

1   tablespoon olive oil, divided

2   cups chicken broth
    (homemade or canned)

Freshly ground pepper to taste

½ to 1 cup milk

2   small leeks, well-washed and quartered

Preheat oven to 375 to 400° F. Cut squash into quarters and place, cut side down, in a baking dish. Bake until just tender, about 30 minutes. Remove from oven, scoop out flesh and set aside. There should be about 3 cups of squash.

In medium pot, sauté onion and carrots in 2 teaspoons olive oil. Add squash and broth. Cover pot and cook for 20 minutes.

Purée, small quantities at a time, in a blender or food processor. Season with pepper. Return soup to pot, reheat and add milk to achieve desired consistency. In a small skillet heat remaining olive oil. Add leeks and sauté until crisp. Garnish soup with leeks. ✹

# TOMATO PEPPER SOUP WITH CROSTINI

SERVES 6

*A beautiful soup to enjoy when red peppers are at their peak.*

2½  pounds (about 4 large) red bell peppers

3  tablespoons olive oil

1  large onion, chopped (1 cup)

3  pounds (about 6 large) tomatoes, peeled, seeded and diced

2  teaspoons sugar

2½ cups beef broth (homemade or canned)

2  bay leaves

½  teaspoon salt

¼  teaspoon pepper

2  tablespoons dry sherry

1  tablespoon sherry wine vinegar

¼  teaspoon hot pepper sauce

## CROSTINI

6  slices sourdough bread

3  tablespoons olive oil

3  tablespoons unsalted butter, melted

2  teaspoons grated lemon peel

¼  teaspoon dried thyme

¼  teaspoon dried basil

¼  teaspoon dried oregano

Prepare roasted red pepper purée according to instructions on page 75 and set aside.

Heat oil in a heavy 4-quart saucepan over medium-high heat. Add onion and sauté until soft, about 8 minutes.

Add tomatoes and sugar and cook, covered, 10 minutes. Stir in broth, bay leaves, salt and pepper. Bring mixture to boil. Cover, reduce heat and simmer 30 minutes. Cool slightly. Discard bay leaves.

Purée tomato mixture, small quantities at a time, in blender or food processor. Return mixture to saucepan. Stir in pepper purée, sherry, vinegar and hot pepper sauce. Gently simmer soup over low heat 20 minutes, stirring occasionally. Ladle soup into serving bowls and top with crostini.

**TO PREPARE CROSTINI,** position rack in center of oven and preheat to 400° F. Place wire cooling rack on large rimmed cookie sheet.

Cut crusts from bread. Cut bread slices in half on diagonal, forming triangles.

Combine remaining ingredients in small bowl. Brush bread on both sides with herb mixture. Place on rack on cookie sheet. Bake until golden brown and crisp, about 10 minutes. ❀

**Note:** *Crostini can be prepared 4 hours ahead and reheated at serving time.*

79

*Soups*

# PURÉE OF CARROT SOUP

SERVES 6

1 large onion, chopped (1 cup)

4 tablespoons (½ stick) butter

1 pound carrots, shredded

5 cups chicken broth (homemade or canned)

⅓ cup uncooked rice

3 shallots, minced

1 teaspoon dried chervil (or 1 tablespoon fresh parsley)

Salt and freshly ground pepper to taste

¾ cup heavy cream

¼ cup sour cream

¼ teaspoon freshly grated nutmeg

In a heavy-bottomed saucepan, sauté onion in butter until soft. Add carrots and toss over medium heat for 3 to 4 minutes. Add chicken broth and bring to boil. Add rice, shallots, chervil or parsley, and salt and pepper. Cover and simmer for 30 minutes, until the carrots fall apart and the rice is overcooked.

Purée through a conical strainer. (Do not use a blender or food processor as it may become gummy.) Bring back to a boil and blend in the creams. Cook until very warm but do not boil. Correct seasoning, add nutmeg, and serve.

# CORN SOUP

MAKES ABOUT 5 CUPS

*The simple solace of creamy bisque.*

3 tablespoons butter

1 medium onion, chopped (½ cup)

2½ cups corn (combination of cream-style and whole kernel)

3 cups milk (or half-and-half), divided

1½ teaspoons salt

Freshly ground pepper to taste

1 tablespoon flour

3 tablespoons chopped fresh parsley

In a heavy-bottomed saucepan melt butter and sauté onion just until softened. In a blender or food processor, purée corn, ½ cup of milk, onion, salt, pepper and flour. Put through a food mill.

Return puréed mixture to saucepan. Add remaining milk and chopped parsley. Cook until thickened, stirring frequently. Serve hot or cold.

# CREAM OF TOMATO SOUP IN PUFF PASTRY

SERVES 8

*Served in ovenproof soup crocks, this makes an elegant presentation.*

## SOUP

1   pound (about 4 medium) yellow onions,
    peeled and chopped

4   tablespoons (½ stick) unsalted butter

3   pounds (about 6 to 8 large) fresh ripe
    tomatoes, quartered (add 1 tablespoon
    tomato paste if tomatoes are not ripe)

6   cloves garlic

1   bay leaf

1   sprig fresh thyme (or ¼ teaspoon dried)

Salt and freshly ground pepper to taste

3   cups heavy cream

## PUFF PASTRY

2   pounds puff pastry*

1   egg beaten with 1 tablespoon water

1   carrot, thinly julienned

1   leek, thinly julienned

½   small onion, cut into very thin rings

Cook yellow onions with butter in a heavy-bottomed 3-quart saucepan over medium heat until soft. Add tomatoes, garlic, bay leaf, thyme and salt and pepper and continue to cook uncovered over low heat for 3½ hours.

Remove bay leaf and purée mixture, small quantities at a time, in a blender or food processor. Strain. Add heavy cream and check seasoning, adding more salt and pepper if necessary. Set aside.

TO PREPARE PASTRY TOPPING, roll puff pastry out to ⅛-inch thickness. Brush surface with egg-wash and reserve remaining wash. Using a sharp knife, cut circles of pastry about 2 inches larger in diameter than the ovenproof soup crocks in which the soup will be served. Pour cooled soup into crocks.

Divide julienned carrots, onions and leeks among the crocks. Lay a circle of puff pastry, egg-wash side down, on top of crock and stretch it tight across the top and attach to sides.

Cover and refrigerate crocks for 1 hour. Preheat oven to 450° F. Brush reserved egg-wash over pastry top. Bake for 15 minutes, or until light brown. Do not open oven during baking, or the pastry will fall. Serve immediately. ❂

**Note:** *Individual soup crocks covered with puff pastry can be prepared 1 or 2 days in advance and refrigerated.*

* *Puff pastry can be found in frozen foods section of most supermarkets.*

# YELLOW PEA AND SPINACH SOUP

SERVES 6 TO 8

1   medium onion, chopped (½ cup)

2   teaspoons minced garlic

2   teaspoons olive oil

1   cup yellow split peas, rinsed

4   cups chicken broth
    (homemade or canned)

2   cups water

1   (10-ounce) package frozen chopped
    spinach, thawed

½   teaspoon salt

⅛   teaspoon pepper

Cook onion and garlic in olive oil in large heavy-bottomed saucepan, covered. Add peas, broth and water. Bring to a boil, then lower heat, cover and simmer for 30 minutes. Add spinach, salt and pepper. Simmer another 30 minutes. ✺

# CAULIFLOWER CARAWAY SOUP

SERVES 4

1   pound cauliflower, sliced thin,
    reserving 1 cup flowerettes for garnish

½   onion, sliced

5   tablespoons butter, divided

2   teaspoons caraway seeds, ground

3   cups chicken broth
    (homemade or canned)

2   teaspoons fresh lemon juice

Freshly ground pepper to taste

2   plum tomatoes, peeled, seeded
    and chopped

1   tablespoon minced fresh parsley

In a small saucepan of boiling water blanch the reserved 1 cup cauliflower flowerettes for 3 minutes and drain.

In a large heavy-bottomed saucepan sauté the onion in 4 tablespoons butter over low heat, stirring until softened. Add caraway seeds, broth, sliced uncooked cauliflower and bring to boil. Cover and cook mixture over moderately low heat until cauliflower is tender, about 20 minutes.

In blender or food processor, purée the mixture, small quantities at a time. Return purée to large saucepan and keep warm. Add lemon juice and pepper.

Cook tomatoes in a small skillet with 1 tablespoon butter, stirring, for 5 minutes. To serve, pour soup into bowls and garnish with a spoonful of tomatoes and reserved flowerettes. Sprinkle with parsley. ✺

Note: Soup can be made one day ahead. Cover and refrigerate. Reheat gently and garnish before serving.

# GOLDEN CLAM CHOWDER

SERVES 6 TO 8

3   slices bacon

6   scallions, chopped

5   medium Idaho potatoes, peeled and diced

3   (6½-ounce) cans chopped clams

3   carrots, shredded

4   cups milk

2   cups bottled clam juice

⅓   cup dry white wine

1   teaspoon salt

½   teaspoon white pepper

In a heavy-bottomed saucepan fry bacon until crisp and remove. Sauté scallions in bacon grease until soft. Add potatoes, clams, carrots and simmer 10 minutes. Add milk, clam juice and wine and simmer, covered, until vegetables are tender. Season with salt and pepper. Garnish with crumbled bacon. ❀

# TOMATO AND CRABMEAT SOUP

SERVES 4 TO 6

3   pounds (6 to 8 large) ripe tomatoes, peeled, seeded and chopped, about 6 cups

1   large red onion, chopped (1 cup)

1   red bell pepper, chopped

1   tablespoon minced garlic

2   teaspoons chopped jalapeño pepper or to taste

6   tablespoons coarsely chopped fresh cilantro, divided

4   tablespoons olive oil

2   tablespoons red wine vinegar

3   tablespoons fresh lime or lemon juice

Salt and freshly ground pepper to taste

1½ cups peeled, seeded cucumbers cut into ¼-inch cubes

1   pound lump crabmeat, shells and cartilage removed

Combine all the ingredients except for 2 tablespoons of the cilantro, the cucumbers and the crabmeat in a food processor or blender, and blend to a semi-coarse texture. Pour the mixture into a bowl. Cover with plastic wrap and refrigerate until cold.

Stir in the cucumbers and crabmeat just before serving. Serve in chilled bowl, and sprinkle with the remaining 2 tablespoons of cilantro. ❀

# VEGETABLES

*Detail from a 19th century Turkoman*

*table cover made in Central Asia*

*from traditional geometric-floral patterning.*

# SWEET AND SAVORY EGGPLANT

SERVES 4

*A smooth and unusual accompaniment to grilled beef, lamb or chicken — more than a condiment, not quite a vegetable side dish, this richly colored eggplant relish disappears quickly.*

1   medium eggplant (1¼ pounds),
    cut into 1-inch cubes

1   medium onion, cut into ¼-inch slices

1   clove garlic, minced

2   teaspoons curry powder

1   teaspoon grated fresh ginger

6   tablespoons peanut oil

½   teaspoon salt

2   teaspoons fresh lemon juice

2   tablespoons mango chutney

Put eggplant into bowl and add onion, garlic, curry powder and ginger. Toss to mix.

In large skillet, heat oil over high heat and when very hot add eggplant mixture. Sauté, tossing frequently, for about 3 minutes.

Reduce heat to moderate and cook, tossing frequently, until eggplant is tender and browned, about 25 minutes.

Remove from heat and stir in salt, lemon juice and chutney. Serve at room temperature. 🌿

# EGGPLANT GRATIN

SERVES 4 TO 6

2   medium eggplants (about 2½ pounds)

3   tablespoons olive oil

3   cups tomato sauce

5   tablespoons minced fresh herbs,
    preferably a mixture of basil, thyme
    and Italian parsley

Salt and freshly ground pepper to taste

Preheat oven to 450° F. Peel and cut each eggplant lengthwise into slices ⅛-inch thick.

Use a pastry brush to brush the slices on each side with olive oil and place them on an oiled baking sheet. Bake until light brown on one side, 5 to 10 minutes. Turn and bake until light brown on other side, about 5 more minutes. Check eggplant frequently and remove slices to a plate as they brown.

Cover bottom of a shallow, 5-cup gratin dish with a thin layer of tomato sauce. Sprinkle with minced herbs and cover with a layer of eggplant slices. Season lightly with salt and pepper. Continue in this manner until all ingredients are used, ending with a layer of tomato sauce. Bake until crispy and bubbly, about 30 minutes. Serve warm or at room temperature. 🌿

# CRISPY EGGPLANT (a favorite from the original *Artist in the Kitchen*)

SERVES 4 TO 5

*The eggplant miracle.*

1   medium eggplant (1¼ pounds)
Salt
½   cup fine bread crumbs
¼   cup freshly grated Parmesan cheese
Salt and freshly ground pepper to taste
Mayonnaise

Preheat oven to 425° F. Slice eggplant ¼ to ½-inch thick. Lightly salt and let drain on towel for 30 minutes. Rinse well and pat dry.

Mix crumbs and cheese. Add salt and pepper. Spread both sides of drained eggplant with mayonnaise. Coat both sides with crumb mixture. Place eggplant on greased cookie sheet and bake for 15 minutes. You do not need to turn eggplant; it will brown on both sides.

# COLD RED PEPPER AND TOMATO GRATIN

SERVES 6

*This is a blissful summer union of peppers and tomatoes. A useful make-ahead dish.*

2 to 3   red bell peppers
6   large, firm, ripe tomatoes, in season
2   tablespoons olive oil, divided
½   cup fresh Italian parsley leaves, minced
1   tablespoon dried thyme
1   tablespoon capers
2   tablespoons bread crumbs (preferably homemade)
⅓   cup fresh basil, chopped

Prepare roasted red peppers according to instructions on page 75. Cut into 1-inch strips.

Preheat oven to 350° F. Wash tomatoes and slice each into 4 round pieces.

Grease an earthenware or enamel casserole dish with 1 tablespoon olive oil and cover the bottom with ⅓ of the tomato slices.

Mix together parsley and thyme. Sprinkle tomatoes with ⅓ of this herb mixture. Cover with half of the pepper strips. Repeat the layering, ending with tomatoes.

Sprinkle the top with capers and bread crumbs and drizzle with remaining olive oil. Bake 20 minutes. Chill. Sprinkle with chopped basil before serving.

# RED AND GREEN PEPPERS WITH ANCHOVIES AND CAPERS

SERVES 4 TO 6

*This flavorful side dish is a colorful accompaniment to simple grilled meat or chicken.*

3   tablespoons olive oil

2   red bell peppers, cut into ½-inch strips

2   green bell peppers, cut into ½-inch strips

3   cloves garlic, minced

1   (3-ounce) can anchovies, chopped
    (reserve oil)

4   tablespoons capers

2   teaspoons dried oregano

1   tablespoon red wine vinegar

1   teaspoon freshly ground pepper

Heat olive oil in a large heavy skillet and add peppers and garlic. Cook over medium heat 3 to 5 minutes, stirring continuously.

Add anchovies and reserved oil and cook 2 minutes, continuing to stir.

Add capers and oregano, cooking 2 more minutes. Sprinkle with red wine vinegar and pepper. May be served warm or at room temperature.

# ELEGANT CARROTS

SERVES 4

*One purée sure to bring compliments.*

4   large carrots, peeled and cut in rounds
    (about 2 to 2½ cups)

1 to 2 tablespoons butter or margarine

1   tablespoon Grand Marnier or other
    orange liqueur

Salt and freshly ground pepper to taste

Place carrots in a saucepan with water and cook until tender, about 20 minutes. Drain. Reserve a cup of the cooking liquid to add later to the purée to achieve desired consistency. Purée in food processor or blender with butter, Grand Marnier, salt and pepper.

**Note:** *This recipe can be made with yams as well. Substitute bourbon for Grand Marnier.*

# SNOW PEAS WITH CARROTS AND RED PEPPER

SERVES 4

1   tablespoon unsalted butter or margarine

2   medium carrots, peeled and cut
    into julienne

1   medium sweet red bell pepper, cored
    and peeled, cut into julienne

¾   pound snow peas or sugar snap peas,
    trimmed and strings removed

¼   teaspoon grated lemon peel

1   teaspoon fresh lemon juice

⅛   teaspoon black pepper

Melt butter over moderate heat in a heavy skillet. Add carrots and red pepper and cook, covered, for 3 minutes. Add snow peas, cover and cook 2 minutes longer or just until vegetables are tender. Stir in lemon peel, lemon juice and black pepper and serve immediately.

# CURRIED NEW POTATOES AND GREEN ONIONS

SERVES 8

*The welcome crunch of mustard seeds and the pungent enhancement of curry powder put a fresh twist on an old standby. Increase cooking time if you prefer more "crust."*

3   pounds small, red thin-skinned
    potatoes, scrubbed

½ to 1 cup (1 to 2 sticks) butter or margarine

2   teaspoons curry powder

2   teaspoons mustard seeds

2   cups chopped green onions or scallions
    (including tops)

*Salt and freshly ground pepper to taste*

In a 5- or 6-quart pan, cover potatoes with water and bring to a boil. Reduce heat and simmer, covered, until potatoes are tender, but not soft, about 20 to 30 minutes. Drain and let cool. (At this point, you may cover and refrigerate until next day.)

Coarsely chop unpeeled potatoes. Melt ½ cup of the butter in a large heavy frying pan over medium-high heat. Add potatoes and cook, turning frequently with a wide spatula, for about 5 minutes. Add more butter as needed to prevent sticking.

Sprinkle curry powder and mustard seeds over potatoes and mix in. Continue to cook, stirring often, until potatoes begin to brown lightly. Mix in onions or scallions. Season with salt and pepper and serve immediately.

# POTATOES TARRAGON

*Simplicity itself, and a fine accompaniment to roasted meat or fowl.*

2  pounds red potatoes, thinly sliced

4  tablespoons (½ stick) butter

Salt and freshly ground pepper to taste

1  tablespoon fresh parsley, finely minced

1  tablespoon fresh tarragon, finely minced

Sour cream (optional)

Preheat oven to 425° F. Generously grease a round glass pie dish. Pat sliced potatoes dry and cover bottom of dish with a layer of potatoes. Dot with butter, sprinkle with salt and pepper. Sprinkle on ⅓ of parsley and tarragon. Repeat process until dish is full, using all the potatoes, herbs and butter. Cover the dish with another of the same size and put it in the oven. Bake it for 30 minutes.

Take off the cover, reduce the heat to 375 to 400° F. and continue to cook until potatoes are well done and nicely browned on the bottom. This should take 25 to 30 minutes.

Loosen the potatoes around the edge of the dish using a spatula if necessary. Cover the dish with a large round serving platter. Turn over. Potatoes should come out nicely browned on the top. Serve immediately with dollop of sour cream if desired.

# ONION AND GARLIC MASHED POTATOES

SERVES 8

*This is a rich satisfying dish in which the melting onions provide a subtle textural contrast to the velvety potatoes.*

10  tablespoons (1 stick plus 2 tablespoons)
    unsalted butter, divided

1½  pounds onions, thinly sliced

6   cloves garlic, minced

8 to 10 medium-size potatoes
    (Yukon Gold or Russet are best),
    peeled and cut into large chunks

1   cup milk

½   cup heavy cream

1½  teaspoons salt

1¼  teaspoons freshly ground pepper

Sauté the onions in 5 tablespoons butter over low heat, stirring occasionally, until soft. Stir in the remaining butter and the garlic and cook about 10 minutes more; set aside. Meanwhile, boil the potatoes in a covered saucepan about 15 to 20 minutes, until tender. Drain well and gently pat dry. Mash potatoes with a potato masher or squeeze through a ricer to remove lumps. Beat in the milk and heavy cream until thoroughly combined and fluffy. Add the onions, garlic, salt and pepper.

# CRISP POTATOES PANCETTA

SERVES 4

*Hearty, easy, and delicious.*

4   large unpeeled potatoes, well-scrubbed
    and patted dry

4   red bell peppers

2   large yellow onions

4   cloves garlic, minced

½   pound pancetta (Italian bacon)*,
    thinly sliced and chopped

½   cup olive oil

1   teaspoon dried rosemary
    (or 1 tablespoon fresh)

1   teaspoon dried thyme
    (or 1 tablespoon fresh)

Salt and freshly ground pepper to taste

Preheat oven to 400° F. Cut potatoes, peppers and onions into bite-sized pieces. Set peppers aside. Place potatoes and onions in a large bowl and toss with garlic, pancetta, olive oil and seasonings.

Spread mixture evenly in a single layer in a 9 x 13-inch baking pan or on rimmed cookie sheet. Place in oven for 30 minutes, stirring and turning after 15 minutes.

Add pepper pieces and cook another 20 to 30 minutes, stirring and turning every 10 to 15 minutes. When done, vegetables and pancetta will be crisp and brown.

\* Found in specialty food stores. (If regular bacon is substituted it must be cooked until almost crisp and added to potato mixture for last ten minutes of cooking.)

# FRIED SWEET POTATO SLICES

SERVES 8

*Keep sweet potatoes on hand for this dish. It will spruce up even the lowliest of leftovers and may be prepared in minutes.*

5   medium sweet potatoes, peeled and cut
    into medium-thin rounds (approximately
    ⅜-inch)

*Safflower oil for frying (¼-inch deep)*

*Mixed granulated sugar and cinnamon
to taste*

Heat oil in large heavy skillet. Fry potato rounds until golden. Cook quickly but carefully, so as not to burn potatoes. Remove to paper towel and drain. Put on serving platter and, if desired, sprinkle generously with sugar-cinnamon mixture. Serve immediately.

# CORN PUDDING WITH DILL AND PARSLEY

SERVES 4 TO 6

*An excellent pudding in its own right and useful for left-over corn on the cob.*

6   ears white or yellow sweet corn or
    2 (17-ounce) cans corn, drained

½   cup milk

4   eggs

¾   cup cream, warmed

3   ounces Monterey Jack or Muenster
    cheese, grated

1   tablespoon fresh finely chopped dill

1   tablespoon fresh finely chopped parsley

½   teaspoon salt

½   cup toasted plain bread crumbs

Preheat oven to 325° F. Shave kernels from corn with knife. Set aside 1 cup of kernels, and put the rest in a blender with the milk and make a fairly smooth purée.

In a large bowl, beat eggs well. Stir corn purée, corn kernels, cream, cheese, dill, parsley and salt into eggs.

Grease a large baking dish, or 1 cup ramekins with butter, and coat liberally with bread crumbs. Add the corn mixture and set in a deep pan, adding enough water to come halfway up the sides. Bake pudding for about 1 hour 10 minutes if it is in a single dish, 50 to 55 minutes if using the smaller ramekins.

When the top is firm and lightly browned, remove the pudding from the oven and let it rest a few minutes before serving.

# CONFETTI CORN FRITTERS

MAKES 12 FRITTERS

1½  cups whole-kernel sweet corn

2   red bell peppers, finely chopped

1   cup finely chopped scallions

1   teaspoon minced hot green pepper
    such as jalapeño (optional)

1   teaspoon ground cumin

1¼  cups flour

2   teaspoons baking powder

Salt and freshly ground pepper to taste

1   cup milk

4   tablespoons vegetable oil, divided

Mix corn in a bowl with peppers, scallions and hot pepper. Combine dry ingredients and stir into vegetables. Add milk and blend thoroughly.
Heat 2 tablespoons oil in a non-stick skillet. Spoon about ¼ cup of the batter for each fritter in the skillet and cook about 1 to 2 minutes or until golden brown on one side. Turn the fritters and cook about 2 minutes on the second side. Continue until all batter is used, adding more oil as necessary. Serve immediately.

**Note:** *Vegetables can be prepared ahead and refrigerated. Mix with batter shortly before cooking.*

# WINTER VEGETABLE PURÉE

1½  cups peeled and diced carrots

1½  cups peeled and diced turnips

1½  cups peeled and diced rutabagas

2  cups peeled and diced celery root

2  cups peeled and diced parsnips

1  medium sweet potato, peeled and sliced

½  cup (1 stick) unsalted butter, softened

3  tablespoons heavy cream

3  tablespoons brown sugar

In a large saucepan, bring 6 cups of water to a boil. Add the vegetables and cook until tender, about 30 to 40 minutes. Drain. Transfer the vegetables to food processor or blender and purée until smooth. Add the butter, cream and sugar. Process until mixture is smooth and serve. 🌿

**Note:** *The purée can be made up to 24 hours in advance and refrigerated. To serve, place it in a buttered casserole and reheat in a 350° F. oven until hot.*

# BAKED LEEKS

SERVES 6

*Leeks are the true aristocrats of the onion family, easily recognized as such in this simple presentation.*

6  medium to large leeks

1  tablespoon melted butter or margarine

*Freshly ground pepper to taste*

2  tablespoons freshly grated
    Parmesan cheese

Preheat oven to 350° F. Trim base and tough green leaves from leeks, leaving tender green and white parts. Beginning at top green part, cut leeks lengthwise about three-quarters down; spread leaves apart and wash under cold running water.

In large pot of simmering water, cook leeks, covered, for 10 minutes or until tender when pierced with a knife; drain and arrange in single layer in baking dish. Brush with butter and season with pepper to taste; sprinkle with Parmesan.

Cover with foil. (Leeks can stand at room temperature for a few hours or be refrigerated up to 24 hours.) Cover and bake for 25 minutes. 🌿

# WALLA WALLA SWEETS (a favorite from the original *Artist in the Kitchen*)

SERVES 6 TO 8

4   tablespoons (½ stick) butter

7½  cups thinly sliced sweet onions

1   teaspoon salt or more to taste

½   cup rice

¾   cup grated Swiss cheese

⅔   cup half-and-half

Preheat oven to 350° F. In a large skillet or saucepan melt butter and sauté onions until soft but not brown.

Cook rice in 5 cups salted boiling water for 5 minutes only. Drain. Mix onions and rice with cheese and half-and-half. Put in casserole, cover and bake for 50 minutes. Remove cover, place under broiler 3 to 4 minutes or until top is golden brown.

# COLD ASPARAGUS WITH MUSTARD VINAIGRETTE

SERVES 4

*Great for fresh asparagus or a stunning rerun for leftover asparagus.*

20  medium asparagus stalks, trimmed and peeled

1   tablespoon chopped shallot

2   tablespoons balsamic vinegar (or 1½ tablespoons red wine vinegar mixed with ½ teaspoon honey)

2   tablespoons grainy mustard

3   tablespoons canola oil

4   large fresh basil leaves, chopped

Put enough water into a large skillet to fill it 1-inch deep and bring to a boil. Add asparagus, lower heat and cook, covered, until tender-crisp (5-6 minutes). Remove from heat, drain and refresh under cold water. Drain and refrigerate.

In a small bowl, mix together the chopped shallot and balsamic vinegar. Let sit for about 15 minutes. Stir in the mustard. Add oil in a slow, thin stream, whisking vigorously. Add basil and set aside.

At serving time, arrange the asparagus on individual plates or a large serving plate. Whisk the vinaigrette again and pour it over the stalks.

# SPINACH SAUTÉED WITH GARLIC

SERVES 4

*Spinach the Italian way!*

2   pounds fresh spinach

2   cloves garlic, minced

3   tablespoons olive oil

Salt to taste

Crushed red pepper flakes to taste

Wash spinach several times to remove all sand. Drain and cook in covered pan in the water clinging to its leaves. Cook briefly, so that the spinach still retains its bright green color. Remove from pan, drain and chop.

In a sauté pan, heat garlic in olive oil. Do not let garlic brown. Add spinach and sauté briefly. Season to taste with salt and red pepper flakes.

**Note:** *Spinach can be washed early in the day, bagged and refrigerated until preparation time.*

# ITALIAN GREEN BEANS

SERVES 4

½   cup pine nuts

2   ounces thinly sliced pancetta (Italian bacon)*

1   shallot, peeled and minced

¼   cup balsamic vinegar

4   tablespoons (½ stick) unsalted butter

1   pound fresh green beans

Salt and freshly ground pepper to taste

2   tablespoons minced fresh parsley or basil

Preheat oven to 300° F. Spread pine nuts on a shallow baking sheet and toast until pale brown, about 10 minutes.

Fry pancetta in batches in a large skillet over medium heat until crisp. Drain on paper towel. Combine shallot and vinegar in the skillet. Boil over medium-high heat until the liquid is reduced by half. Cut the butter into chunks and whisk in.

Bring a large pot of salted water to a rolling boil. Drop the green beans into the boiling water and blanch for 2 to 3 minutes, until tender but still crisp. Drain well, then transfer to the skillet. Cook over low heat tossing until well coated with butter mixture, about 2 to 3 minutes. Season with salt and pepper to taste. Pour beans into a serving bowl and sprinkle with pine nuts and parsley or basil. Toss to mix. Crumble the pancetta on top and serve hot.

*\* Found in specialty food stores. (Regular bacon may be substituted.)*

# BROILED TOMATOES

SERVES 6

3   large ripe tomatoes

1   clove garlic, minced

1   small onion, finely chopped (¼ cup)

Salt and freshly ground pepper to taste

3   large basil leaves, minced

2   tablespoons brown sugar

2   tablespoons Dijon mustard

6   tablespoons (¾ stick) butter, divided

¾   cup fresh bread crumbs

Preheat broiler. Remove the core from each tomato and slice in half, horizontally. Sprinkle each half with a combination of garlic, onion, salt, pepper and basil. Mix brown sugar and mustard and drizzle over halves. Top each half with a small pat of butter, using about 4 tablespoons in all. Broil for about 5 minutes until bubbly and brown and remove from oven. At this point, tomatoes may sit until final cooking.

Melt remaining 2 tablespoons of butter and toss with bread crumbs. Spread out on baking sheet and bake at 350° F. about 15 minutes until lightly toasted and crisp.

Thirty minutes before serving, sprinkle crumbs on tomatoes and bake at 350° F. about 30 minutes.

# ZUCCHINI PANCAKES

SERVES 4

*Great with grilled pork chops.*

3   cups grated zucchini

1   egg, beaten

¼   teaspoon ground nutmeg

Salt and freshly ground pepper to taste

½   cup flour

1   teaspoon baking powder

3   tablespoons butter

Freshly grated Parmesan cheese to taste

Combine grated zucchini, egg, nutmeg, salt and pepper in a large bowl. Sift flour and baking powder over zucchini and mix well.

Drop mixture by ¼ cupfuls onto lightly greased hot griddle. Cook until golden brown on both sides. Serve, topped with melted butter or dot with butter and cheese.

# RATATOUILLE

SERVES 6

2   large eggplants or 6 small ones

Salt

8   tablespoons olive oil, divided

3   medium onions, finely chopped
    (1½ cups)

6   tomatoes, quartered and seeded

4   cloves garlic, minced

2   bay leaves, divided

2   teaspoons dried thyme, divided

Freshly ground pepper to taste

3   yellow or red bell peppers,
    cut in 1-inch strips

6   zucchini, cut in 1-inch slices

½   cup dry white wine

1   cup chopped fresh basil

Juice of 1 lemon

Peel the large eggplants, or if using small ones, leave them unpeeled. Cut the eggplants in 1-inch slices and cut the slices from the large eggplants in halves. Put them in a colander, salt them, and leave them to drain for 30 minutes. Rinse, press them down and blot with paper towels. Set aside.

Heat 1 tablespoon of the oil in a heavy-bottomed skillet. Add the onions, tomatoes, garlic, 1 bay leaf, 1 teaspoon of thyme, salt and pepper to taste. Cook for 10 minutes, or until the sauce thickens a bit. Pour the sauce into a bowl.

Clean the skillet with a paper towel and heat 3 tablespoons of oil in it. Add the eggplant and sauté 5 minutes. Put in the bowl with the tomato-onion sauce.

Clean the skillet and heat 2 tablespoons more oil in it. Add the peppers, cook stirring frequently over medium-high heat for about 5 minutes. Add the zucchini and stir and cook 5 more minutes.

Pour the entire bowl of cooked vegetables on top of the zucchini and sprinkle with remaining thyme. Add wine, bay leaf and stir well. Simmer uncovered, stirring occasionally, for 1 hour.

Before serving, remove bay leaves and carefully pour off excess liquid. Mix basil and lemon juice into mixture. Serve warm or cold.

**Note:** *The flavor of this dish is improved when prepared 1 or 2 days ahead of serving.*

# CARROT-POTATO PANCAKES

3   medium baking potatoes, peeled

3   eggs, lightly beaten

¼   cup milk

⅓   cup flour

½   teaspoon salt

¼   teaspoon pepper

¼   teaspoon ground nutmeg

2 to 3 carrots, peeled and shredded

1   medium onion, finely chopped (½ cup)

⅓   cup minced fresh parsley

½   cup sour cream

Shred potatoes and place in ice water to cover. Stir together eggs, milk, flour, salt, pepper and nutmeg. Drain potatoes and squeeze out any excess liquid. Add potatoes, carrots, onion and parsley to egg mixture and stir together gently with a spoon.

Drop by spoonfuls on lightly greased hot griddle and flatten each spoonful to a 4-inch circle. Turn when bottom is well browned. Serve with sour cream.

**Note:** *Delicious served with ham or pork roast.*

# VEGETABLE STIR FRY

SERVES 4

*Glistening crisp vegetables quickly prepared.*

2   cups broccoli flowerettes

1   cup cauliflower flowerettes

½   cup scallions or leeks, chopped

30  snow peas

1   red bell pepper, cut in bite-sized pieces

1   cup sliced zucchini

1   tablespoon dried tarragon

1   teaspoon dried basil
    (or 1 tablespoon fresh, minced)

3   cloves garlic, minced

1½  teaspoons salt

¼   cup olive oil

¼   cup vegetable oil

Mix together all vegetables and seasonings in a bowl. Heat oils in wok or large heavy skillet over medium-high heat. When oil shimmers, add vegetables and cook, stirring frequently, about 3 to 5 minutes. Remove from heat and serve immediately.

# FRESH VEGETABLE CHILI

SERVES 6

*A jewelled vegetable medley of crisp flavors and assertive spice. A good dish for late September when peppers are plentiful and the first nip of fall is in the air. Try serving with cheesy cornbread (p.46) and a light green salad.*

| | |
|---|---|
| 1 | *eggplant, cut into ¼-inch pieces* |
| 1 | *tablespoon salt* |
| ½ | *cup olive oil, divided* |
| 1 | *large onion, cut into ¼-inch pieces* |
| 1 | *red bell pepper, cut into 1¼-inch pieces* |
| 1 | *yellow bell pepper, cut into ¼-inch pieces* |
| 1 | *long red hot pepper, seeded, cut into ¼-inch pieces* |
| 6 | *medium cloves garlic, minced* |
| 8 | *ripe plum tomatoes, cut in cubes* |
| 1 | *cup sliced carrots* |
| 1 | *cup water* |
| 1 | *cup dry red wine* |
| 1 | *cup slivered fresh basil leaves* |
| 1 | *tablespoon chili powder* |
| 1 | *tablespoon cumin* |
| 1 | *teaspoon freshly ground black pepper* |
| ¼ | *teaspoon crushed red pepper flakes* |

*Salt to taste*

| | |
|---|---|
| 1 | *(15-ounce) can black beans, drained* |
| 1 | *cup fresh or frozen corn kernels* |
| 1 | *bunch fresh cilantro, washed and chopped* |
| ¼ | *cup fresh lemon or lime juice* |

**Garnish suggestions:** *sour cream, grated Cheddar or Monterey Jack, 4 scallions, thinly sliced (include green tops) or Tomato Salsa (see recipe p. 30)*

Place eggplant in colander and sprinkle with salt. Allow to stand for at least 30 minutes. Rinse and pat dry.

Heat ¼ cup olive oil in large deep skillet. Cook eggplant until tender over medium heat, about 10 minutes. Remove eggplant and set aside.

Place remaining oil in skillet and cook onions, peppers and garlic over medium heat until soft, approximately 10 minutes, stirring frequently. Return eggplant to pan. Add tomatoes, carrots, water, wine, basil and spices. Simmer over low heat for 25 minutes, stirring frequently.

Add beans and corn and cook for an additional 15 minutes. Add cilantro and cook for 2 minutes. Stir in lemon or lime juice. Adjust seasoning. Serve hot, garnished as desired. 🌿

# MUSHROOM FLAN

SERVES 6 TO 8

9-inch pie crust

2  pounds mushrooms

½  cup (1 stick) butter

2  tablespoons chopped shallots

Juice of ½ lemon

¼  cup dry Madeira or sherry

1  tablespoon flour

1  teaspoon salt

½  teaspoon pepper

2  cups heavy cream

1  egg, beaten

½  teaspoon dried thyme

2  tablespoons chopped fresh parsley

¼  cup freshly grated Parmesan cheese

Prepare pie crust according to instructions on page 32 or use favorite recipe, bake and set aside.

Preheat oven to 350° F. Roughly chop mushrooms. Put in corner of tea towel, a handful at a time, and squeeze out excess moisture.

Heat butter in skillet and cook shallots for 3 minutes, stirring. Do not let them brown.

Add chopped mushrooms and lemon juice. Cook, stirring until mixture looks dry, about 10 to 15 minutes.

Add Madeira and cook until it evaporates. Sprinkle flour, salt and pepper over mushrooms and stir. Beat egg into cream and add to mushroom mixture. Cook until mixture is very thick, about 15 to 20 minutes; add thyme.

Pour into baked shell and sprinkle with parsley and Parmesan cheese. Bake for 15 minutes.

**Note:** *May be assembled ahead and frozen. Defrost at room temperature.*

# BAKED CREAMY ZUCCHINI

(a favorite from the original *Artist in the Kitchen*)

SERVES 4

6 to 8 small zucchini

1   (3-ounce) package cream cheese

3   tablespoons butter

2   cloves garlic, minced

Round butter crackers

Preheat oven to 350° F. Peel and grate zucchini. Squeeze all moisture out of grated zucchini by wrapping in a clean dish towel and pressing liquid out.

Melt cheese and butter and mix with garlic. Combine zucchini with butter/cheese mixture. Put in a baking dish and crumble crackers on top. Bake for 25 minutes until golden brown.

# SAGE AND ONION STUFFING CASSEROLE

SERVES 4

½   pound minced raw veal, pork or turkey

4   tablespoons (½ stick) butter, divided

3   large onions, finely chopped (3 cups)

1   egg

1   cup milk

10 fresh sage leaves, finely chopped (or 3 teaspoons dry)

2   cups fresh white bread crumbs made from dense bread like Italian

6   tablespoons slivered almonds, divided

1   teaspoon salt

½   teaspoon freshly ground pepper

Preheat oven to 350° F. Sauté minced veal, pork or turkey in 1 tablespoon butter. When meat is nicely browned, remove it from pan and set aside.

Add remaining butter to same pan and sauté the onions until they are soft. In a large bowl, beat the egg. Add milk, meat, onions and remaining ingredients, reserving 2 tablespoons almonds.

Place the stuffing in greased 1½-quart baking dish; sprinkle with the remaining almonds. Bake 40 minutes or until it starts to brown. Serve with roast chicken or grilled meat.

# FISH & SEAFOOD

Detail from a silk kente cloth wrapper

worn for ceremonial purposes by the

Asante people in Ghana, West Africa.

# SHRIMP WITH ROSEMARY

SERVES 4

24 large shrimp (2 pounds), rinsed

5 tablespoons olive oil, divided

1 small onion, chopped (¼ cup)

½ medium carrot, diced

1 shallot, diced

1 medium leek, well-washed and diced

1 medium tomato, diced

¼ fennel bulb, diced

½ tablespoon tomato paste

¼ cup Cognac

1 cup dry white wine

1 cup clam juice

1 clove garlic, minced

3 tablespoons fresh rosemary, divided

10 peppercorns

Salt and freshly ground pepper to taste

Sprigs of fresh rosemary

Shell and devein shrimp. Refrigerate shrimp. Boil shrimp shells in 3 cups cold water for 20-25 minutes to create shrimp stock. Set aside.

In large saucepan, sauté onion, carrot, shallot, leek, tomato and fennel in 2 tablespoons oil for about 5 minutes until vegetables are soft but not brown.

Add tomato paste and stir until blended. Add Cognac and white wine. Simmer on low heat until all liquid is absorbed, about 45 minutes.

Add 1 cup shrimp stock, clam juice, garlic, 1 tablespoon rosemary and peppercorns. Simmer 30 minutes. Strain and salt to taste. Set aside and keep warm.

Butterfly shrimp. Season with salt and pepper. Heat a saucepan and add the remaining 3 tablespoons olive oil. Place shrimp split side down in the pan and cook until golden brown, about 4 minutes. Do not overcook.

Just before shrimp are done, sprinkle on 2 tablespoons of rosemary. Spoon rosemary sauce over shrimp, garnish with rosemary sprigs and serve immediately.

# SCAMPI SAUTÉ

SERVES 2 TO 3

*A quick supper to serve over rice or pasta.*

1  tablespoon coarse sea salt or Kosher salt

1  pound medium shrimp (about 20),
   peeled and deveined

½  cup olive oil

1  tablespoon minced garlic

½  teaspoon crushed red pepper flakes

1  teaspoon dry sherry vinegar
   or white wine vinegar

¼  cup finely chopped fresh parsley

In a medium bowl, stir salt into 1 cup of water until dissolved. Add shrimp and let soak for 5 minutes. Drain and pat dry.

In a heavy skillet, heat oil over moderately high heat until hot but not smoking. Add shrimp in 1 layer and sprinkle with garlic and red pepper. Cook shrimp, turning once, about 1 minute per side. Do not overcook. Stir in vinegar and parsley and serve. 🔲

# SKEWERED GRILLED SHRIMP

SERVES 4

2  pounds large shrimp peeled or unpeeled*,
   deveined, rinsed and patted dry

½  cup (1 stick) butter, melted

½  cup olive oil

4  cloves garlic, minced

¼  teaspoon crushed red pepper flakes

1  teaspoon salt

2  tablespoons snipped fresh chives

2  tablespoons minced fresh parsley

2  tablespoons minced fresh basil
   (or 2 teaspoons dried)

1  teaspoon freshly ground pepper

¼  cup fresh lemon juice

3  red bell peppers, cut in 1-inch squares

2  large white onions, cut in chunks

If leaving shells on shrimp, cut through shell first with scissors to remove the vein. Place cleaned shrimp in a large bowl.

Combine butter, olive oil, garlic, red pepper flakes, salt, chives, parsley, basil, pepper, lemon juice and pour over shrimp. Marinate 1 to 2 hours, no longer.

Skewer shrimp with pepper and onions and brush with marinade. Grill over medium hot coals (or broil in oven) about 3 minutes per side. Heat remaining marinade about 1 to 2 minutes until it boils and serve with the shrimp. 🔲

* *The shrimp are more flavorful with the shells left on during cooking and serving, but a bit messy. Pass the napkins!*

# SEA SCALLOPS WITH ZUCCHINI AND RED PEPPERS

SERVES 4

*A light and very easy preparation for scallops. Lovely as a first course served sandwiched between a split, commercially prepared puff pastry.*

2   tablespoons olive oil, divided

2   tablespoons butter, divided

2   red bell peppers, cut into ½-inch cubes

1   cup zucchini, cut into thin slices

¼   teaspoon Tabasco

Salt and freshly ground pepper to taste

1½  pounds sea scallops, rinsed
    and patted dry

2   cloves garlic, minced

1   teaspoon fresh thyme
    (or ½ teaspoon dried)

2   tablespoons dry vermouth

1   tablespoon fresh lemon juice

4   tablespoons coarsely chopped fresh basil
    or tarragon (or 2 teaspoons dried)

In a large nonstick skillet or wok, heat 1 tablespoon of the olive oil and 1 tablespoon of the butter over medium heat.

Add the red peppers and the zucchini and cook, stirring for 5 minutes. Add Tabasco, salt and pepper and continue to cook vegetables until tender-crisp.

Add the remaining butter and olive oil and stir in the scallops, garlic, thyme, vermouth, lemon juice and basil.

Cook over high heat, stirring 3 to 5 minutes until the scallops are heated through. Do not overcook. Serve immediately.

# Scallops in Red Pepper Purée

SERVES 6

*Tender scallops in a beautiful, rich pink sauce.*

## PURÉE

2   tablespoons butter

1   pound red bell peppers, diced
    (about 2 large peppers)

1   tablespoon sugar

1   tablespoon cider vinegar

½   teaspoon paprika

¼   teaspoon crushed red pepper flakes

## SCALLOPS

2   tablespoons butter

2½  pounds sea scallops, rinsed
    and patted dry

1   cup dry white wine

¼   cup dry sherry

1   cup heavy cream

Salt and freshly ground pepper to taste

In a heavy saucepan, melt butter over low heat. Add peppers, sugar, vinegar, paprika and pepper flakes and stir to combine. Cover and steam over low heat for 45 minutes or until peppers are soft.

Uncover, increase heat and cook until peppers are lightly browned and all liquid is evaporated. Do not let peppers burn.

Purée in a blender or food processor until smooth. (Purée can be made in advance and refrigerated 1 or 2 days or frozen for longer.) Makes about ½ cup.

Heat the butter in a large heavy skillet. Add scallops and sauté about 3 minutes. Remove scallops and set aside.

Add wine and sherry to skillet. Cook over high heat until liquid is reduced and thickened, about 5 to 10 minutes.

Add cream and cook another 2 to 3 minutes. Stir in pepper purée. Add scallops and cook gently until warm throughout. Serve with rice.

**Note:** *For a lighter version substitute chicken broth and/or wine for the heavy cream.*

# SALMON WITH GINGERED VEGETABLES

SERVES 4 TO 6

*This recipe is low in calories, high in flavor and extremely easy.*

1½-pound salmon fillet, rinsed and patted dry

1   cup dry vermouth or dry white wine

Salt and freshly ground pepper to taste

2½ tablespoons butter, divided

2   teaspoons oriental sesame oil

2   large leeks (white part only),
    well-washed and thinly sliced

3   carrots, peeled and sliced on diagonal

2   teaspoons grated fresh ginger

1   large clove garlic, minced

Preheat oven to 350° F. Score skin side of salmon fillet and place skin side down in buttered baking dish. Salt and pepper fillet to taste.

Pour vermouth or wine around salmon (it should be about ¼ inch to ½ inch deep in pan).

Butter a sheet of waxed paper with ½ tablespoon butter and place it butter side down on the salmon. Poach in oven for 15 to 20 minutes. (Do not overcook. Salmon should be pale pink in the center.)

While salmon is cooking, heat remaining butter and sesame oil in a large skillet. Add leeks, carrots, ginger and garlic and sauté until vegetables are tender, 5 to 10 minutes.

When done, remove salmon from oven, reserving cooking liquid and place on warm serving platter. Top with sautéed vegetables. Keep warm.

Place cooking liquid in skillet. Boil over high heat reducing it until shiny and syrupy. Pour sauce over salmon and serve.

# GRILLED SALMON STEAKS WITH MUSTARD MINT SAUCE

SERVES 6

*This very piquant sauce is a surprisingly perfect companion for the tender salmon steaks.*

6   salmon steaks, cut 1-inch thick, rinsed
    and patted dry

Salt and freshly ground pepper to taste

3   tablespoons olive oil

SAUCE

1½ tablespoons Dijon mustard

1½ tablespoons coarsely ground pepper

3   tablespoons white wine vinegar

¼   cup chopped fresh mint

¾   cup olive oil

Rub steaks with olive oil and sprinkle with salt and pepper. Cook in preheated broiler or grill about 5 or 6 minutes per side.

**TO MAKE SAUCE,** purée mustard, pepper, vinegar and mint in a blender or food processor. Add oil in a slow steady stream. Makes about 1 cup. Serve sauce at room temperature with salmon steaks.

# SALMON CAKES

MAKES 12 SALMON CAKES. SERVES 6

1½ pounds fresh salmon steaks, each about
    1-inch thick (or 3 cups flaked, canned
    salmon, skin and bones removed)

2   eggs, lightly beaten

1¼ cups fine fresh crumbs made from
    unsalted crackers, divided

½   teaspoon paprika

Salt and freshly ground pepper to taste

¼   cup finely chopped chives

2   tablespoons finely chopped fresh parsley

⅛   teaspoon freshly grated nutmeg

6   tablespoons vegetable oil

Lemon wedges

Put salmon steaks into the rack of a steamer. Place the rack over boiling water and cover closely. Let steam 7 minutes.

When fish is cool enough to handle, remove and discard skin and bones. Flake the fish. There should be about 3 cups. Put fish in a mixing bowl and add eggs, 1 cup of the crumbs, paprika, salt, pepper, chives, parsley and nutmeg. Blend, leaving flaked fish in fairly large lumps.

Shape the mixture into 12 cakes of equal size. Coat the cakes on all sides with the remaining crumbs. Heat about 2 tablespoons of oil in a heavy skillet for each batch of cakes to be fried. Add a few cakes at a time and cook about 2½ minutes on each side or until golden brown on both sides. Drain on absorbent paper towels. Serve hot with lemon wedges.

# SALMON PROVENÇAL

SERVES 4

*Gusty provençal flavors in counterpoint to the tart and creamy goat cheese create a lively and colorful dish.*

4   tablespoons olive oil, divided

1   medium onion, chopped (½ cup)

1   tablespoon minced garlic

½   cup dry red wine

4   tablespoons capers

1   tablespoon chopped fresh rosemary
    (or 1 teaspoon dried)

1   teaspoon chopped fresh oregano
    (or ½ teaspoon dried)

⅛   teaspoon crushed red pepper flakes

½   cup canned crushed tomatoes

Salt and freshly ground pepper to taste

12  pitted imported black olives
    (Kalamata or Italian)

4   boneless salmon fillets or salmon steaks,
    about 6 ounces each, rinsed and
    patted dry

⅓   pound goat cheese, crumbled

2   tablespoons anise-flavored liqueur,
    like Pernod

4   tablespoons chopped fresh cilantro

Heat 2 tablespoons of the olive oil in a saucepan. Add the onion and garlic, and cook just until soft. Add the wine, capers, rosemary, oregano, pepper flakes, tomatoes, salt, pepper and olives. Bring to a boil and simmer 5 minutes.

Preheat oven to 475° F. Pour 1 tablespoon of the oil in a baking dish large enough to hold the fish in one layer. Arrange the fish skin-side down, sprinkle with salt and pepper.

Pour the tomato sauce around the fish fillets, brush the top of the fillets with the remaining 1 tablespoon oil. Sprinkle the cheese over the top. Bake for 5 minutes and sprinkle with Pernod.

Switch to the broiler and broil for 5 minutes. Do not overcook the fish. Sprinkle with cilantro and serve immediately.

**Note:** *Bluefish is also excellent prepared in this manner.*

# MARINATED SWORDFISH WITH PINEAPPLE SALSA

SERVES 4 TO 6

2   pounds swordfish steaks, cut 1-inch thick

MARINADE

½   cup vegetable oil

¼   cup soy sauce

¼   cup fresh orange juice

¼   cup fresh lemon juice

2   teaspoons freshly grated lemon peel

2   tablespoons grated fresh ginger

6   cloves garlic, minced

SALSA

1½ cups chopped fresh pineapple

1   small red onion, chopped (¼ cup)

1   medium red bell pepper, cored, seeded and diced

½   teaspoon canned or bottled minced jalapeño pepper

2   tablespoons chopped fresh cilantro

2   tablespoons fresh lime or lemon juice

1   large clove garlic, minced

2   teaspoons minced fresh ginger

½   teaspoon ground cumin

1   teaspoon freshly ground black pepper

Combine all ingredients for marinade. Arrange swordfish steaks in large glass baking dish, prick in several places with a fork and cover with marinade. Refrigerate for 1 to 3 hours, turning at least twice.

TO MAKE SALSA, combine all ingredients in glass bowl or measuring cup, cover and chill preferably for 2 hours or longer.

Grill steaks 6 minutes per side, brushing frequently with marinade, or cook 5 to 6 minutes per side in hot skillet using 1 tablespoon butter and 2 tablespoons olive oil. Serve with Pineapple Salsa.

**Note:** *Salsa is also excellent with tuna, shrimp or grilled chicken.*

*Fish
&
Seafood*

# GRILLED TUNA STEAKS WITH SUN-DRIED TOMATOES AND FRESH CORN

SERVES 4

*The tomatoes and corn furnish strong bursts of color and flavor.*

4   (6-ounce) tuna steaks, rinsed
    and patted dry

¼   cup corn oil

2   teaspoons coarsely chopped shallots

2   cloves garlic, minced

2   teaspoons fresh oregano leaves
    (or ½ teaspoon dried)

2   bay leaves

½   teaspoon crushed black peppercorns

3   tablespoons diced sun-dried tomatoes

⅔   cup raw sweet corn kernels

4   fresh basil leaves

Place tuna in shallow glass dish and sprinkle with oil, shallots, garlic, oregano, bay leaves and crushed peppercorns. Let sit 1 hour at room temperature, turning fish several times.

Remove fish from the marinade, reserving marinade, and place on hot grill or under broiler and cook 5 to 6 minutes per side. As tuna cooks, quickly sauté reserved marinade in small saucepan until garlic is soft.

Add tomatoes and corn and cook 3 minutes, or until corn is cooked through. Place grilled steaks on plates and top with the tomato-corn mixture. Garnish with basil leaves.

# MAHI-MAHI WITH MACADAMIA NUTS

SERVES 2

3   tablespoons butter, divided

2   (6-ounce) fillets mahi-mahi
    (or other delicate white-fleshed fish),
    rinsed and patted dry

*Flour*

1   tablespoon Kosher salt

2   tablespoons coarsely diced
    macadamia nuts

*Juice of 1 lime*

Melt 2 tablespoons of the butter in heavy pan. Dust fish lightly on both sides with flour. Sauté fish about 3 minutes on each side over medium heat. Season to taste with salt and set aside on a warm platter.

Add remaining tablespoon of butter to pan and heat until golden. Add the nuts and cook, stirring, about 10 seconds. Add the lime juice. Stir and drizzle over fish.

# BAKED RED SNAPPER WITH FETA

SERVES 4

2½ pounds red snapper fillets, rinsed
    and patted dry

2   tablespoons olive oil

1   small onion, chopped (¼ cup)

2   teaspoons minced garlic

1   (14½-ounce) can tomatoes

2   tablespoons tomato paste

2   tablespoons drained capers

1   teaspoon dried oregano

¼   teaspoon crushed red pepper flakes

6   tablespoons minced fresh parsley, divided

Salt and freshly ground pepper to taste

¼   pound crumbled Feta cheese

Preheat oven to 425° F. Arrange the fish in a single layer in a baking dish. Set aside.

Heat the oil in a sauté pan. Add onions and cook until they start to wilt. Add garlic and continue cooking a few minutes more. Add tomatoes with their liquid, tomato paste, capers, oregano, red pepper and 4 tablespoons of parsley. Cook, uncovered, over medium heat about 10 minutes until sauce is slightly thickened.

Pour sauce over fish. Bake, uncovered, 15 minutes. Sprinkle with cheese and bake 5 minutes longer. Sprinkle with remaining parsley and serve at once.

**Note:** *Other mild white-fleshed fish fillets like fluke, sea bass or flounder may be substituted very successfully.*

# BLUE BLUEFISH

SERVES 4

4   medium bluefish fillets, rinsed
    and patted dry

4   teaspoons fresh lemon juice

4   tablespoons dry white wine

4   tablespoons dried plain bread crumbs

4   tablespoons crumbled blue cheese

Freshly ground pepper to taste

4   teaspoons butter

Preheat oven to 375° F. Place bluefish fillets on greased baking pan. Sprinkle lemon juice and wine evenly over all. Sprinkle each fillet with a tablespoon of bread crumbs and a tablespoon of blue cheese. Season with pepper and dot each fillet with a teaspoon of butter.

Bake for approximately 15 minutes, depending on the thickness of the fillets, until lightly browned and bubbling.

# CRAB CAKES WITH MUSTARD SAUCE

MAKES 16 TO 18 SMALL CAKES.
SERVES 3 AS A MAIN COURSE OR 6 TO 8 AS AN APPETIZER.

*What a treat for a rainy Sunday!*

½ pound sea legs

2 tablespoons mayonnaise

1 tablespoon heavy cream

2 teaspoons Dijon mustard

1 teaspoon fresh lemon juice

½ teaspoon Worcestershire sauce

¼ teaspoon salt

⅛ teaspoon cayenne pepper

¼ teaspoon oriental sesame oil

2 tablespoons chopped fresh cilantro or parsley

¼ cup chopped scallions, including green part

1 tablespoon olive oil

1 egg

1½ cups fine, fresh bread crumbs, divided

1 (6½-ounce) can good quality crabmeat

Corn, peanut or vegetable oil for frying

Lemon wedges

## MUSTARD SAUCE

1 teaspoon dry mustard

⅓ cup mayonnaise

¼ cup sour cream

¾ teaspoon Worcestershire sauce

1 tablespoon heavy cream

⅛ teaspoon Tabasco sauce

1 teaspoon ketchup (optional)

Salt to taste

**TO MAKE CRAB CAKES,** put all the ingredients except ½ cup of bread crumbs and crabmeat in the bowl of a food processor and pulse to mix.

Transfer to a medium bowl and gently mix in the crabmeat, leaving lumps whole.

Shape the mixture into portions of equal size. Shape in flat patties. Coat each patty with the remaining bread crumbs, cover and chill until ready to cook.

The crab cakes may be cooked in deep fat heated to 360° F. for 2 to 3 minutes or until golden brown all over. Or they may be cooked in a heavy skillet in 3 tablespoons of oil for each batch of cakes to be fried. Add a few cakes at a time and cook over medium-low heat about 2 to 2½ minutes on each side or until golden brown on both sides. Drain on absorbent paper towels. Serve hot with lemon wedges and mustard sauce.

**TO MAKE THE MUSTARD SAUCE,** combine mustard and mayonnaise in a small bowl. Beat by hand for 1 minute until smooth. Add remaining ingredients and beat until creamy. Cover and chill for at least 1 hour.

**Note:** *Sauce is also excellent with roast beef sandwiches or as a dip for crudités with the addition of fresh herbs sprinkled on top.*

# CIOPPINO

*Serve this hearty fish stew with lots of fresh French bread for dipping.*

½ cup olive oil

1½ teaspoons minced garlic

3 medium onions, chopped (1½ cups)

¾ cup chopped green bell pepper

2 teaspoons chili powder

1 (14½-ounce) can Italian tomatoes with juice

1 tablespoon tomato paste

2 cups clam juice

1½ cups dry red wine

2 teaspoons dried oregano

½ teaspoon dried basil

1½ pounds halibut, skinned and cut into chunks

1 pound shrimp, peeled, deveined and rinsed

1 pound scallops, rinsed

Salt and freshly ground pepper to taste

Heat olive oil in heavy pot and add garlic, onion, green pepper and chili powder. Sauté until onions are translucent. Add tomatoes, tomato paste, clam juice, wine, oregano and basil. Simmer for 15 minutes.

Just before serving, bring the soup to a low boil and add the fish. Cook about 5-10 minutes. Add salt and pepper.

*115*

**Fish**
**&**
**Seafood**

# POULTRY

*Detail from a coverlet woven by an*

*itinerant weaver in Pennsylvania in the*

*19th century showing oriental design*

*influences in the border.*

# PAELLA

SERVES 6

¼   cup olive oil

1   (1½ to 2 pound) chicken, cut into pieces,
    washed and patted dry

Salt and freshly ground pepper to taste

½   pound hot chorizos (Spanish sausage),
    thinly sliced

1   medium onion, thinly sliced

1½  cups rice

1   teaspoon saffron

3   cups chicken broth (homemade
    or canned)

1 or 2 cloves garlic, minced

1   (9-ounce) package frozen
    artichoke hearts

1   large tomato, peeled and diced

1   pound shrimp, peeled and deveined

6   small hard-shelled clams, scrubbed

6   small mussels, scrubbed and
    beards removed

½   cup cooked peas

½   cup canned chick peas, rinsed
    and drained

3   slices pimento

2   lemons, cut into wedges

Heat the olive oil in a heavy skillet or paella pan. Season chicken with salt and pepper and cook over medium heat until nicely browned.

Remove from pan and set aside. Cook chorizos and onion in same pan until onion is soft, but not brown. Add rice, cook a couple of minutes, stirring.

Dissolve saffron in a little hot chicken broth. Add 3 cups of broth including dissolved saffron and stir until it comes to a boil.

Add garlic, place chicken on top. Cover and cook over very low heat for about 20 minutes.

Break up artichokes and put them with chopped tomato around rice.

Cover and simmer for another 15 minutes. Add shrimp, pushing well down into rice. Add clams and mussels and cook another 5 minutes or until they open, discarding any that do not open during cooking.

Sprinkle peas and chick peas over all and garnish with pimento strips. Serve with lemon wedges.

# FRENCH COUNTRY CHICKEN

SERVES 6

½  pound bacon, cut into ½-inch pieces

12  small new potatoes

2  (3-pound) chickens, washed and patted dry, cut into serving pieces

Salt and freshly ground pepper to taste

2  tablespoons unsalted butter

3  tablespoons olive oil

6  medium carrots, trimmed, peeled and sliced

20 to 25 tiny pearl onions

4  cloves garlic, minced

1  bay leaf

6  sprigs parsley, chopped

3 to 4 sprigs fresh thyme, chopped

Preheat oven to 375° F. Blanch bacon in boiling water for 3 minutes; drain, refresh with cold water and pat dry.

Peel potatoes and blanch for 5 minutes; drain and pat dry. Trim fat from chicken, and season with salt and pepper.

Add butter and oil to a large covered casserole and brown chicken over high heat; remove and set aside.

Add bacon to pot and brown; remove. Brown carrots and remove. Brown pearl onions and remove. Brown blanched potatoes and remove.

Pour off excess fat and return chicken to casserole. Add bacon, vegetables, garlic, bay leaf, and parsley and thyme. Pour in ½ cup water and season with additional salt and pepper.

Bake, covered, for 1 hour and 15 minutes.

119

**Poultry**

# GRILLED CITRUS CHICKEN JALAPEÑO

SERVES 6

6  boneless, unskinned chicken breasts
   (about 2½ pounds), washed and
   patted dry

Peanut, corn or vegetable oil for greasing
the grill

## MARINADE

4  oranges

2  limes

1  lemon

2  large onions, finely chopped (2 cups)

4  cloves garlic, minced

3½ tablespoons finely diced, seeded
   jalapeño peppers

1  tablespoon finely chopped fresh sage
   (or 1 teaspoon dried)

¾  cup finely chopped fresh parsley,
   loosely packed

1  cup loosely packed, coarsely chopped
   fresh cilantro

1  cup olive oil

TO PREPARE THE MARINADE, use a sharp knife to peel away the zest or thin outer layer of two of the oranges and one of the limes and the lemon. Set aside. Squeeze the four oranges, the two limes and the lemon. Set juices aside.

Put the onions, garlic and jalapeño pepper into the container of a food processor and blend briefly. Do not purée. Add the zest of the oranges, the lime and the lemon. Pulse about 10 times until blended. Add the orange, lime and lemon juices, sage, parsley, cilantro and the olive oil. Blend thoroughly, about 1 minute.

Pour half the marinade in the bottom of a dish large enough to hold the breast halves in one layer. Place the breast halves skin-side up in the dish. Spoon the remaining marinade over. Let stand, covered, 2 hours at room temperature.

When ready to cook, preheat grill to medium. Brush grill evenly with oil. Place breast pieces skin-side down on the grill. Brush the top of each half with a little of the marinade.

Cook 10 minutes. Remove the pieces from the grill and dip them in the marinade. Return the pieces, skin-side down, to the grill for 5 minutes longer. Dip the pieces once more in the marinade and arrange the pieces skin-side up on the grill. Continue cooking 5 to 10 minutes longer, depending on the thickness of the pieces.

# GRILLED CHICKEN "QUATORZE"*

SERVES 8 TO 12

*A lot of steps but worth it! Great flavor.*

3  (3-pound) chickens, washed and patted
    dry, cut into 6 pieces each

## MARINADE

½  ounce fresh marjoram**
    (about ½ cup packed)

½  ounce fresh oregano**
    (about ½ cup packed)

½  ounce fresh thyme**
    (about ½ cup packed)

10  cloves garlic

¼  cup dried thyme

¼  cup dried oregano

10  bay leaves

Juice of 3 lemons

2  tablespoons salt

½  teaspoon ground white pepper

1½ cups olive oil

**TO PREPARE THE MARINADE,** mince the fresh herbs and garlic. Place in the bowl of a food processor with the dried herbs, bay leaves, lemon juice, salt and pepper. With the machine running, slowly pour in the olive oil to form a thick emulsion.

Combine the chicken pieces with this marinade in a non-aluminum bowl or pan, cover with plastic wrap, and refrigerate 2 or 3 days, turning chicken pieces occasionally.

When ready to cook, drain the chicken. In a sauté pan over medium-high heat, briefly sear chicken on both sides, a few pieces at a time. Place the pieces in a shallow roasting pan and roast uncovered in a preheated 400° F. oven for about 20 minutes, or until almost cooked through.

Remove the chicken pieces with tongs, and place over a hot grill for about 5 to 7 minutes, turning several times. ✳

\* Adapted from Quatorze bis Restaurant, New York.

\*\* 1/2-ounce packages of fresh herbs are found in the produce sections of most supermarkets.

# Grilled Chicken with Peach Salsa

SALSA MAKES 3 CUPS. CHICKEN SERVES 6 TO 8

8  boneless, skinless breasts of chicken,
   washed and patted dry

## MARINADE

¾  cup olive oil

½  cup fresh lemon juice

½  cup any combination of fresh herbs
   such as rosemary, tarragon, thyme, or
   sage, minced

2  cloves garlic, minced

Salt and freshly ground pepper to taste

## PEACH SALSA

2  cups peeled, diced ripe peaches
   (about 2 large peaches)

1  medium onion, chopped (½ cup)

½  cup diced red bell pepper

½ to ¾ teaspoon minced jalapeño
   or serrano chili

2  teaspoons olive oil

2  tablespoons fresh lime juice

¼  cup minced fresh mint

2  teaspoons grated fresh ginger

**To prepare the marinade,** combine olive oil, lemon juice, herbs, garlic, salt and pepper. Place chicken in a non-aluminum shallow dish and pour marinade over. Cover and marinate in refrigerator at least 2 hours, turning occasionally.

While chicken marinates combine all ingredients for salsa and set aside.

Broil chicken in oven or grill on barbecue about 5 minutes per side. Serve with peach salsa.

**Note:**  Salsa is also a delicious accompaniment to grilled swordfish.

122

# DAY AHEAD CURRY MUSTARD CHICKEN

(a favorite from the original *Artist in the Kitchen*)

SERVES 4 TO 6

4 to 6 boneless chicken breasts (with or
    without skin), washed and patted dry

½  cup honey

½  cup Dijon mustard

1  tablespoon curry

2  tablespoons soy sauce

Place chicken snugly in baking dish, skin side down.
Mix honey, mustard, curry and soy sauce. Pour over
chicken and refrigerate for 6 hours or overnight, covered.

When ready to cook, preheat oven to 350° F.

Turn chicken over. Cover with foil and bake 1 hour.
Remove cover, baste well and continue baking for
15 minutes. Place chicken on a platter and spoon sauce
over to serve. ✼

# BARBECUED CHICKEN IN SPECIAL SAUCE

(a favorite from the original *Artist in the Kitchen*)

SERVES 12

*A nice alternative to the standard tomato-based barbecue.*

6  (1½-pound) broiler chickens, cut into
    pieces, washed and patted dry

Salt and freshly ground pepper to taste

5  ounces prepared yellow mustard

5  ounces Worcestershire sauce

Juice of 3 lemons

Grated peel of 3 lemons

2  cups white vinegar

1  pound (4 sticks) butter or margarine

Several hours before barbecuing, season the chicken
with salt and pepper. Refrigerate.

Combine mustard, Worcestershire sauce, lemon juice,
grated peel and vinegar in saucepan. Simmer for
20 minutes. Remove from heat. Add butter or
margarine and allow it to melt.

Grill the chickens over a slow fire, basting frequently
with the sauce. ✼

# CHICKEN TANDOORI STYLE WITH YOGURT SAUCE

SERVES 6

3 pounds chicken pieces, washed and patted dry and cut into pieces

## 1ST MARINADE

½ teaspoon salt

Juice of one lemon

## 2ND MARINADE

1 cup plain yogurt

Juice of one lemon

2 tablespoons vegetable oil

1 tablespoon tomato paste

1 tablespoon flour

1½ teaspoons ground cumin

½ teaspoon ground ginger (optional)

1 small clove garlic, minced (optional)

½ teaspoon celery salt

¾ teaspoon paprika

½ teaspoon ground white pepper

¼ teaspoon ground allspice

## YOGURT SAUCE

2 tablespoons corn oil

1 tablespoon minced fresh ginger

3 cloves garlic, minced

¾ teaspoon curry powder

2 teaspoons ground fennel

½ teaspoon ground cumin

½ teaspoon ground coriander

2 cups plain yogurt

1¼ teaspoons salt

¼ teaspoon pepper

1 teaspoon fresh lemon juice

1 tablespoon chopped fresh cilantro

Remove fat and skin from chicken. Sprinkle with salt and let marinate in a non-aluminum pan or bowl in the lemon juice for two hours.

Combine the ingredients for the second marinade and pour over the chicken. Marinate for a minimum of 16 hours.

Chicken can be cooked in oven or on grill.

If using oven, preheat to 350° F. Place the chicken with the marinade in a shallow baking dish. Bake for 45 minutes. Turn oven to broil, raise chicken to highest rack and broil about 5 minutes to brown nicely.

If cooking on a grill, cover the grill with aluminum foil. Place the chicken on the foil and cook with the lid of the grill closed. If the grill has no lid, cover the chicken with aluminum foil. Turn the meat every 15 minutes and cook until the juice runs clear when the meat is pierced with a fork.

Combine all ingredients for yogurt sauce and serve at room temperature with chicken. Serve with cucumber and tomato salad and warm pita bread.

# CHICKEN PROVENÇAL

SERVES 6

*A robust colorful peasant dish from southern France perfect for a cold winter night.*

2   (2½-pound) broiler chickens, washed, patted dry and cut into pieces

*Juice of 1 lemon*

*Salt and freshly ground pepper to taste*

2   tablespoons butter

1   tablespoon olive oil

2   large onions, chopped (2 cups)

1   cup chicken broth (homemade or canned)

1   cup tomato purée

3   bay leaves

¼   teaspoon each dried saffron, oregano, marjoram, rosemary, thyme, tarragon and fennel

3   large basil leaves, minced (or ½ teaspoon dried)

½   teaspoon black pepper

¾   cup dry white wine or vermouth

4   cloves garlic, minced

½   cup pitted Greek Kalamata olives

Preheat oven to 350° F. Rub the chicken pieces with lemon juice and season with salt and pepper.

Heat the butter and olive oil in a large heavy skillet and brown the chicken. When brown on both sides, remove the chicken to an ovenproof casserole.

In the fat remaining in the pan, cook the onions until soft. Add the rest of the ingredients and simmer for 15 minutes.

Pour the liquid over the chicken, cover and cook in the oven for 30 minutes. Uncover the casserole and continue cooking 15 minutes more.

Serve with crusty bread or rice and a salad.

# CHICKEN BREASTS WITH GOAT CHEESE AND BASIL

SERVES 4

*These are so easy, yet quite elegant. The creamy goat cheese is a delicious complement to the grilled chicken.*

4   boneless chicken breast halves, with skin, washed and patted dry

2 to 4 ounces mild goat cheese

12 to 20 fresh basil leaves

Salt and freshly ground pepper to taste

2   tablespoons olive oil (if sautéing)

**BASIL CREAM SAUCE**

2   shallots, chopped

¾   cup heavy cream

¼   cup chicken broth (homemade or canned)

Approximately 20 fresh basil leaves

Gently pull the skin back and cut a 1 x 2-inch pocket in the meaty center of each breast so that each breast opens like a book. For each breast wrap ½ to 1 ounce goat cheese in 2 or 3 basil leaves, place in pocket and gently close.

Place 1 or 2 basil leaves directly under skin on top side of breasts and close skin over. Season with salt and pepper.

Grill breasts over medium-hot coals 3 to 4 minutes per side or alternately sauté in 2 tablespoons of olive oil about 4 minutes per side. Keep chicken warm.

**TO PREPARE SAUCE,** simmer shallots with cream and broth in medium saucepan until reduced by two-thirds; strain.

Just before serving, julienne basil leaves and stir half of them into sauce.

Serve chicken breasts with basil cream sauce and garnish with remaining julienned basil. ✻

# CHICKEN PAPRIKA

SERVES 4

2  tablespoons butter or vegetable oil

1  tablespoon olive oil

2  large onions, finely chopped (2 cups)

3  tablespoons sweet paprika

Salt to taste (about 1 teaspoon)

¼  teaspoon cayenne pepper

4  boneless skinless chicken breasts, washed
   and patted dry

1  cup heavy cream

24  pearl onions (optional)

4  large fresh mushroom caps (optional)

Sauté chopped onions in butter or oil until tender in a covered sauté pan, approximately 5 minutes. Add paprika, cayenne pepper and salt.

Place chicken breasts on top of the onions, cover and simmer until tender, approximately 10 to 15 minutes. The chicken breasts should be just done, not dry.

Stir the mixture, placing some of the onions on top of chicken breasts. Be sure none of the onions or chicken sticks to pan.

Add the cream to the pan, as well as the pearl onions and the mushrooms if desired, and stir gently; cover and cook until onions and mushrooms are cooked. Serve immediately with rice or pasta. ✳

**Note:** *For a lighter dish, steam the onions in chicken broth until tender and use chicken broth in place of cream for sauce.*

# CHICKEN STIR-FRY WITH EGGPLANT AND ARTICHOKES

SERVES 2 TO 3

4   tablespoons vegetable oil, divided

2   scallions, sliced diagonally into small pieces

1   red bell pepper, cut in 1-inch cubes

2   cloves garlic, minced

½   cup walnuts

1   large whole boneless, skinless chicken breast washed, patted dry and cut into 1-inch pieces

1   tablespoon soy sauce, divided

½   pound eggplant, cut in 1½-inch cubes

½   cup marinated artichoke hearts, drained

2   tablespoons hoisin sauce*

1   tablespoon fresh lemon juice

½   cup chicken broth (homemade or canned)

2   teaspoons cornstarch dissolved in 1 tablespoon broth or water

In wok or heavy-bottomed skillet heat 2 tablespoons of oil. When very hot, add scallions, red pepper, garlic and nuts and stir-fry 30 seconds. Transfer to a large bowl and set aside.

Add 1 tablespoon of oil to the pan. Heat until very hot, add chicken and cook, stirring briskly until browned on all sides, about 2 minutes.

Season with ½ teaspoon soy sauce. Add to nut mixture. Add remaining tablespoon of oil to the pan. When hot, add the eggplant. Stir-fry until well coated.

Season with remaining soy sauce. Lower heat to medium, cover, and cook about 3 minutes, until tender.

Return chicken mixture and any juices to pan. Add artichoke hearts, hoisin sauce, lemon juice and broth. Stir together until artichoke hearts are warm. Adjust seasonings.

Add cornstarch mixture and stir until sauce thickens. Serve immediately with rice or noodles. ✳

* Available in the oriental foods section of most supermarkets.

# ORIENTAL CHICKEN (a favorite from the original *Artist in the Kitchen*)

SERVES 4 TO 6

2  whole boneless, skinless chicken breasts, washed and patted dry

6  tablespoons peanut oil

6  scallions, sliced

1  cup broccoli flowerettes

½  pound fresh mushrooms, sliced

1½ cups diagonally sliced celery

1  red bell pepper, cut in ¼-inch strips

½  cup chicken broth (homemade or canned)

⅓  cup toasted slivered almonds for garnish (optional)

## MARINADE

1  tablespoon cornstarch

2  tablespoons water

3  tablespoons soy sauce

1  tablespoon unsulphured molasses

¼  teaspoon tabasco or red pepper flakes (or more to taste)

1½ teaspoons salt

1  tablespoon grated fresh ginger (or ½ teaspoon dry ginger)

Combine marinade ingredients. Cut chicken breasts into ½-inch strips and marinate for up to 3 hours in refrigerator.

When ready to cook, heat oil in wok or large heavy skillet. When hot, add chicken and marinade, scallions and broccoli. Stir-fry over high heat for 3 to 5 minutes until chicken turns white. Add remaining ingredients and stir-fry another 3 to 4 minutes until vegetables are crisp-tender.

Garnish with almonds if desired and serve with rice.

# Chicken Tetrazzini* (a favorite from the original *Artist in the Kitchen*)

SERVES 6

- 2 *whole chicken breasts, washed and patted dry*
- 1 *small onion, quartered*
- 1 *carrot, sliced*
- 2 *ribs celery, sliced*
- 3 *sprigs fresh parsley*
- 1 *bay leaf*
- ½ *teaspoon salt*
- 3 *whole peppercorns*
- ¾ *cup (1½ sticks) butter, divided*
- ½ *pound fresh mushrooms, sliced*
- ½ *pound cooked ham, in fine strips*
- ½ *pound linguine*
- 1 *cup fresh or frozen peas*
- 2 *cups heavy cream*
- 1 *cup freshly grated Parmesan cheese*

*Minced fresh parsley*

*Salt and white pepper to taste*

Poach chicken breasts in a skillet in water to cover, with onion, carrot, celery, parsley, bay leaf, salt and peppercorns, over medium-high heat about 25 minutes or until tender. Let breasts cool in broth, and when cool, discard skin and bones.

Cut chicken into strips and cover. Strain and degrease broth. Set both aside.

Melt ½ cup butter and sauté mushrooms lightly. Add ham and chicken strips and cook several minutes, stirring. Remove from heat. Set aside.

In a heavy saucepan, bring unsalted water to a boil and add the noodles gradually. Cook until noodles are firm but not soft. Drain and return to saucepan.

Combine chicken mixture with noodles. Add the remaining butter and the peas. Cook briefly to meld flavors. Add cream and simmer until sauce thickens and peas are cooked. Add Parmesan cheese and mix well.

Remove from heat. If sauce is too thick, stir in up to 1 cup of reserved chicken broth. Season with salt and white pepper. Heat but do not allow it to boil. Pour into a heated dish and sprinkle with parsley.

**Note:** *For a change, use green noodles and sautéed shrimp instead of chicken.*

* *Adapted from Tony Bommarito*

# CHICKEN-CHEESE LASAGNA

*A delicious and different lasagna. The noodles cook with the sauce!*

½ cup (1 stick) margarine or butter

2 cloves garlic, minced

½ cup flour

1 teaspoon salt

2 cups milk

2 cups chicken broth (homemade or canned)

2 cups freshly grated Mozzarella cheese

1 cup freshly grated Parmesan cheese, divided

1 medium onion, chopped (½ cup)

1 teaspoon dried basil leaves

½ teaspoon oregano leaves

¼ teaspoon pepper

12 ounces lasagna noodles (12 noodles), uncooked

2 cups creamed cottage cheese

4 cups shredded cooked chicken

2 (10-ounce) packages frozen chopped spinach, thawed and squeezed dry

Heat margarine in 2-quart saucepan over low heat until melted; add garlic. Stir in flour and salt. Cook, stirring constantly, until bubbly. Remove from heat; stir in milk and broth. Heat to boiling, stirring constantly. Boil and stir 1 minute.

Stir in Mozzarella cheese, ½ cup Parmesan cheese, onion, basil, oregano and pepper. Cook over low heat, stirring constantly, until Mozzarella cheese is melted.

Preheat oven to 350° F.

Spread ¼ of the cheese sauce (about 1½ cups) in an ungreased rectangular baking dish, 13 x 9 x 2-inches.

Top with 3 or 4 uncooked noodles, overlapping if necessary. Spread half of the cottage cheese over noodles. Repeat with another ¼ of the cheese sauce, 3 or 4 noodles and remaining cottage cheese.

Top with chicken, spinach, ¼ of the cheese sauce, remaining noodles and remaining cheese sauce. Sprinkle with remaining Parmesan cheese.

Bake uncovered until noodles are done, 35 or 40 minutes or longer. Let stand 15 minutes before cutting. ✽

# CORNISH GAME HENS WITH DRIED FRUIT STUFFING

SERVES 2

1   small onion, chopped (¼ cup)

2   tablespoons butter

½   teaspoon dried thyme

1   tablespoon ground coriander

1   tablespoon dry sherry

1   apple, peeled and cut into ½-inch pieces

6   dried apricots, quartered

6   dried prunes, cut into ½-inch pieces

¼   cup raisins

2   Cornish game hens, washed and patted dry

½   cup dry white wine

Preheat oven to 400° F. Sauté onion in butter until soft.

Combine onion with remaining ingredients (except wine) in a large bowl. Stuff hens with mixture. Place hens in a shallow baking dish and pour the white wine around.

Bake about 45 minutes to 1 hour until nicely browned.

# Cornish Game Hens with Orange Sauce

(a favorite from the original *Artist in the Kitchen*)

SERVES 4

- ½ *cup wild rice*
- 1 *small onion, finely chopped (¼ cup)*
- ¼ *cup fresh mushrooms, chopped*
- 1 *tablespoon butter*
- 3 *tablespoons Burgundy wine*

*Salt and freshly ground pepper to taste*

- 4 *Cornish game hens, washed and patted dry*

ORANGE SAUCE

- 1 *cup fresh orange juice*
- ¾ *cup water*
- ¼ *cup Cognac or sherry*
- 1 *tablespoon sugar*
- ½ *teaspoon salt*
- 2 *tablespoons freshly grated orange peel*
- 1 *orange, peeled and very thinly sliced*
- 1 *tablespoon cornstarch*
- 3 *teaspoons cold water*

Cook rice according to package directions. Sauté onion and mushrooms in butter for 5 minutes over medium-high heat.

Mix cooked rice with onion, mushrooms and wine. Season with salt and pepper. Preheat oven to 350° F. Stuff hens with rice mixture and bake for 45 minutes.

**To make orange sauce,** mix orange juice, water, cognac, sugar, salt, orange peel and slices and simmer for 10 minutes. Blend cornstarch with cold water until smooth. Add to orange sauce, stirring constantly until thickened. To serve, spoon orange sauce over cooked hens and pass extra sauce.

# QUAIL WITH CHESTNUTS AND GRAPES

(a favorite from the original *Artist in the Kitchen*)

SERVES 6

6    quail, washed and patted dry

1    cup cooked chestnuts, mashed

1    cup white seedless grapes

2    tablespoons butter

1    tablespoon vegetable oil

1    medium yellow onion, chopped (½ cup)

2    carrots, chopped

6    slices bacon, fried crisp and crumbled

2    tablespoons flour

1    cup dry red wine

2    tablespoons port wine or Madeira

½    cup chicken broth (homemade or canned)

Salt and freshly ground pepper to taste

Parsley

Preheat oven to 350° F. Stuff quail with as many chestnuts and grapes as they will hold and truss.

In a large sauté pan, heat butter and oil and brown quail lightly. When brown, place them in a large ovenproof casserole.

Sauté onion and carrots in remaining fat in the sauté pan. Add bacon and any remaining chestnuts and grapes. Add flour and stir over low heat about 2 minutes. Stir in wines and broth and cook until the sauce is smooth and thickened. Season with salt and pepper. Pour over quail, cover and bake 45 minutes. Garnish with parsley and serve with wild rice.

# SOUTHWESTERN TURKEY CHILI

SERVES 6

2  cups dried black beans

½  cup (1 stick) unsalted butter

1  cup chopped mild fresh chilies

⅔  cup chopped red onion

⅔  cup chopped celery

⅔  cup chopped red bell pepper

⅔  cup chopped white part of leek

2  cloves garlic, minced

2  tablespoons dried oregano, crumbled

¼  cup flour

4  cups cooked turkey, shredded

4  cups chicken broth (homemade or canned)

2¼ cups corn, divided

2  tablespoons ground coriander

2  tablespoons chili powder

1  tablespoon ground cumin (or more to taste)

Salt and freshly ground pepper to taste

Rinse beans and let soak overnight in water to cover. Drain, combine with 8 cups of water and simmer uncovered for about 1½ hours until tender. Drain and set aside.

Melt butter and cook chilies, onion, celery, pepper, leek, garlic and oregano about 10 to 15 minutes, until softened, stirring occasionally. Add flour and turkey and cook over low heat, stirring, for about 15 minutes. Add broth.

Purée 1¼ cups corn and add to mixture along with rest of corn, coriander, chili powder, cumin, salt and pepper and reserved beans.

Simmer 15 to 20 minutes, correct seasonings and serve. ✳

135

**Poultry**

# DEEP DISH CHICKEN PIE

*This colorful, multi-flavored chicken pot pie is a great do-ahead supper for a crowd.*

1   pound puff pastry*

3   pounds whole boneless, skinless chicken breasts, washed and patted dry

1   cup heavy cream

4   carrots, peeled and sliced diagonally

½   cup (1 stick) unsalted butter, divided

2   leeks (white part only), well-washed and sliced

1   fennel bulb, sliced

1   large red onion, thinly sliced

2   unpeeled Granny Smith apples, cored and sliced

½   pound sugar snap peas, with tops and ends removed

2   zucchini, unpeeled and sliced diagonally

½   cup flour

1   cup chicken broth (homemade or canned)

2   cups apple cider

¼   cup Cognac

3   tablespoons chopped fresh tarragon

2   teaspoons ground coriander

½   tablespoon nutmeg

1   teaspoon allspice

3   cups cooked wild rice (1 cup raw)

Salt and freshly ground pepper to taste

1   egg, beaten with ¼ cup water

Preheat oven to 350° F. If using frozen puff pastry, remove from freezer and set aside.

Place chicken breasts in a single layer in a baking pan. Pour the cream over and bake for 20 to 25 minutes. (Meat will be firm and pink in the center.) Reserve cream and cooking juices.

Cut cooled chicken into 1-inch pieces. Raise oven temperature to 425° F.

Blanch carrots in lightly salted water, about 3 minutes. Rinse in cold water and drain.

Melt ½ stick butter in large skillet over medium heat; add leeks, fennel, and onions and sauté for 10 minutes or until soft. Stir in apples, peas, zucchini and carrots. Cook for 1 to 2 minutes. Remove from heat.

Melt remaining butter in large pot and blend in flour. Cook, stirring constantly, for 5 minutes. Do not burn. Add broth and apple cider and cook, stirring constantly, until thickened, about 10 minutes. Stir in reserved cream, cooking juices and Cognac. Cook over low heat until the mixture thickens, about 10 minutes. Stir in spices. Add chicken, vegetables and rice to cream sauce, mixing gently. Add salt and pepper.

Pour mixture into a large shallow baking dish. On a lightly floured surface, roll out pastry to fit dish. (If pastry comes in more than one sheet, overlap edges slightly.) Place on top of dish, leaving a 1-inch overhang. Brush edge of pastry with egg/water mixture, and press the overhanging dough back onto dish to form a lip around edge of the dough. Cut a steam vent in the center and brush the entire surface with egg/water mixture.

136

*continued next page*

At this point, the pie may be refrigerated until cooking time. If refrigerated add about 15 minutes to the final cooking time.

When ready to cook, place in the center of the oven and bake for 15 minutes. Reduce heat to 350° F. and bake for an additional 35 to 40 minutes, or until crust is deep golden. ✳

**Note:** *This dish may be frozen prior to final baking. If you plan to freeze the pie, substitute baby peas for the sugar snap peas.*

*\* Puff pastry can be found in frozen foods section of most supermarkets.*

# MEATS

*Detail from a rug woven by a nomad*

*in central Turkey in the 19th century.*

# FILLET OF BEEF WITH TWO SAUCES

SERVES 8

*The red and yellow sauces with this beef make for an especially beautiful presentation.*

3½-pound fillet of beef

2   tablespoons vegetable oil

1   large clove garlic, halved

Sea salt or Kosher salt

### RED PEPPER SAUCE

3   cups thinly sliced red bell peppers
    (about 3 large peppers)

2   tablespoons olive oil

1   canned chipotle chili, in adobo,
    unseeded* (or 1 small can chopped
    green chilies)

2   teaspoons Worcestershire sauce

Salt to taste

### MUSTARD CHIVE SAUCE

½   cup dry mustard

3   tablespoons white vinegar

1½ teaspoons sugar

1½ teaspoons salt

3   tablespoons water

6   tablespoons (¾ stick) unsalted
    butter, softened

3   tablespoons snipped fresh chives

Rub the fillet with vegetable oil and with the cut clove of garlic. Roll in sea salt. Cook over charcoal for about 8 minutes per side or until meat thermometer registers 130° F. Serve warm or at room temperature with the sauces.

**TO PREPARE RED PEPPER SAUCE,** cook red peppers in olive oil in a heavy skillet over moderately low heat, covered, stirring occasionally, for about 25 minutes until they are soft. In a blender or food processor, purée the mixture with the chipotle, Worcestershire sauce and salt. Serve the sauce warm or at room temperature. Makes 1 cup.

**TO PREPARE THE MUSTARD SAUCE,** in a small bowl stir together the mustard, vinegar, sugar, salt and water to make a smooth paste. Cover and let stand for 10 minutes. Transfer to top of a double boiler set over barely simmering water and whisk in the butter until just combined. Remove from the heat and stir in the chives. Serve the sauce warm or at room temperature. Makes 1 cup.

* Available in Hispanic markets or specialty food stores.

140

# SAUERBRATEN

SERVES 8 TO 10

*You will want to bring back this traditional piquant winter entrée.*

*4-pound chuck roast*

*Salt and freshly ground pepper to taste*

2   *cups wine vinegar*

2   *cups water*

2   *cloves garlic, peeled*

1   *cup sliced onion*

1   *bay leaf*

10  *peppercorns*

¼   *cup sugar*

3   *whole cloves*

*Flour for dredging and thickening gravy*

2   *tablespoons bacon drippings*

2   *tablespoons flour*

¼   *cup water*

½   *cup sour cream*

Season meat with salt and pepper and place in a large bowl. Bring vinegar and water to a boil and add garlic, onion, bay leaf, peppercorns, sugar, and cloves. Pour marinade over the beef, cover, and refrigerate 12 hours or overnight.

Remove meat and dry thoroughly with paper towels. Reserve marinade. Dredge meat with flour. In a heavy pot heat bacon drippings, add meat, and brown on all sides. Add 2 cups of marinade, cover tightly and simmer gently until meat is tender, 2½ to 3 hours. Remove meat to a warm platter and tent with foil.

Thicken gravy with 2 tablespoons of flour mixed with water. Cook for 5 more minutes. Gradually stir in sour cream, but do not bring to a boil. Serve over the sliced meat. 

*141*

**Meats**

# BEEF BURGUNDY

SERVES 6

*A rich, flavorful stew for a dinner or buffet.*
*Serve this with garlic mashed potatoes and a crisp salad.*

8   tablespoons (1 stick) butter or
    margarine, divided

2½ pounds boneless beef chuck or sirloin tip
    cut into 1½-inch pieces

3   tablespoons brandy

12 to 15 small white onions, peeled

1   pound fresh mushrooms (halved if large)

4 to 6 tablespoons flour

2   teaspoons beef soup base
    (or paste made of two crushed
    bouillon cubes in 2 teaspoons water)

2   tablespoons tomato paste

1½ cups Burgundy

½   cup dry sherry

¾   cup port

1¼ cups beef broth (homemade or canned)

Salt and pepper to taste

1   bay leaf

Preheat oven to 350° F. Melt 2 tablespoons of butter in a large ovenproof pan. Add beef in small batches and brown well. Remove beef as it browns. Continue until all beef is browned, adding more butter as needed. Then return beef to pan.

In a small saucepan, heat brandy. Ignite, and pour over beef. As flames dies, remove beef and juices and set aside.

Melt 2 tablespoons butter in pan. Add onions and mushrooms and cook over low heat, covered, until onions are light brown. Remove onions and mushrooms from pan and set aside.

Stir flour, soup base and tomato paste in pan until well blended. Stir in Burgundy, sherry, port and beef broth and bring to boil, stirring; remove from heat.

Add beef, pepper, and bay leaf; mix well. Cover and bake for 1½ hours, or until beef is tender. Stir occasionally. Add onions and mushrooms during last 30 minutes of baking.

If sauce is too thin, thicken by melting 1 tablespoon butter in saucepan. Stir in 2 to 3 tablespoons flour and cook until mixture is thoroughly combined. Drain sauce from stew pot and whisk into butter/flour mixture a little at a time until blended and smooth. Pour sauce over stew.

**Note:** *This dish is best made a day ahead, refrigerated, and warmed for serving.*

# THREE PEPPER CHILI

SERVES 6

*A chili sophisticated enough for entertaining.*

8    tablespoons (1 stick) butter, divided

2    cloves garlic, minced

2    large onions, finely chopped (2 cups)

1    large green bell pepper, finely chopped

3    large tomatoes, chopped

1    teaspoon sugar

4    fresh whole basil leaves, chopped,
     (or ¼ teaspoon dried)

1    bay leaf, crumbled

1½  pounds ground beef

1    tablespoon vegetable oil

1    beef shoulder steak (1½ pounds),
     fat removed, cut into 2 x ½-inch strips

3    tablespoons chili powder
     (or more to taste)

¼    teaspoon dried thyme

½    teaspoon paprika

½    teaspoon cayenne pepper

½    teaspoon ground allspice

1    dried red chili pepper, crushed

1    teaspoon soy sauce

½    teaspoon hot pepper sauce

6    canned serrano chilies, chopped

½    cup dry red wine

1    cup beef broth (homemade or canned)

1    teaspoon salt

½    teaspoon freshly ground pepper

3    cups cooked red kidney beans

Cooked rice

Sour cream (optional)

Cilantro (optional)

Preheat oven to 300° F. Melt 5 tablespoons butter in heavy skillet. Add garlic, onions and green bell pepper; sauté over medium heat 5 minutes. Add tomatoes; sprinkle with sugar, basil, and bay leaf. Cook 10 minutes more and transfer mixture to an ovenproof pot.

Place ground beef in skillet and cook over high heat until the meat is brown. Transfer to pot.

Add 2 to 3 tablespoons butter and the oil to the skillet; sauté steak over high heat, a few strips at a time, until well browned on all sides. Transfer cooked strips to a plate. Drain skillet. Return steak to skillet; stir in chili powder. Cook over low heat 3 minutes. Transfer to pot.

Stir remaining ingredients (except beans, rice, sour cream and cilantro) into pot and bake, covered, 3 hours.

Stir in beans and bake ½ hour longer. Serve over cooked rice with a dollop of sour cream and a few leaves of cilantro.

**Note:** *Chili may be prepared a day ahead and also freezes well.*

# Marinated Flank Steak

SERVES 6

*Serve this warm or at room temperature. For your family or for company, as a sandwich or a delicious partner for more elaborate vegetables, this flank steak goes everywhere!*

2   large flank steaks

**MARINADE**

½   cup olive oil

¼   cup soy sauce

2 to 3 tablespoons Balsamic vinegar

¼   cup fresh lemon juice

3   tablespoons honey

1   clove garlic, minced

½   teaspoon grated fresh ginger

1½   teaspoons salt

1   teaspoon sugar

2   tablespoons grated onion

½   teaspoon dry mustard

1   teaspoon freshly ground pepper

Place all marinade ingredients in a food processor or blender. Mix until thick and smooth. Pour over flank steaks (in a non-metallic pan) and let stand, covered, in refrigerator from 6 to 24 hours, turning occasionally.

Broil or grill about 5 to 6 minutes per side. To serve, slice thinly, diagonally across the grain.

# Steak Sandwich Deluxe

(a favorite from the original *Artist in the Kitchen*)

SERVES 4

*A great treat for a stay-at-home dinner.*

4   slices French or Italian bread,
    about ½-inch thick

4   tablespoons (½ stick) butter, divided

1½-pound beef tenderloin, cut in 4 slices

Salt and freshly ground pepper to taste

½   cup port wine

2   tablespoons heavy cream

Brown the bread on both sides in a hot skillet in 2 tablespoons of melted butter. Remove the bread and set aside. Add the remaining butter to the skillet and brown the meat 3 minutes on each side. Season with salt and pepper and place on top of bread. Stir port into pan and cook until wine is reduced by half. Stir in cream and simmer 1 or 2 minutes, stirring constantly, until the sauce thickens. Pour the sauce over the sandwiches and serve at once.

# RACK OF LAMB WITH WILD MUSHROOM SAUCE

SERVES 4 TO 6

2   *racks of lamb, about 2½ pounds combined weight*

4   *tablespoons (½ stick) butter, divided*

*Salt and freshly ground pepper to taste*

½   *cup bread crumbs*

2   *tablespoons chopped parsley*

1   *clove garlic, minced*

1   *shallot, minced*

1   *teaspoon olive oil*

## WILD MUSHROOM SAUCE

1   *ounce dried wild mushrooms such as cèpes or Porcini (available at specialty food stores)*

1   *pound fresh mushrooms, coarsely chopped*

2   *tablespoons butter*

¾   *cup heavy cream*

*Salt and freshly ground pepper to taste*

¼   *teaspoon freshly grated nutmeg*

⅛   *teaspoon cayenne pepper*

Have a butcher prepare two fully trimmed racks of lamb leaving the bones as long as possible.

Preheat broiler to high. Grease baking dish large enough to hold both racks of lamb in 1 layer. Place racks, meat side down, in dish and dot with 2 tablespoons butter, salt and pepper. Place racks under the broiler and cook 2 to 3 minutes. Turn and cook 2 to 3 minutes more.

Meanwhile, combine bread crumbs, parsley, garlic, shallot and olive oil in bowl. Spread bread-crumb mixture on meaty side of ribs. Melt remaining 2 tablespoons butter and pour over ribs. Set oven at 400° F. Place in oven and bake 15 to 20 minutes, depending on degree of doneness desired.

**TO PREPARE MUSHROOM SAUCE**, bring 2½ cups of salted water to a boil and add dried mushrooms. Cook about 1 minute. Drain immediately extracting as much liquid as possible, and coarsely chop. Sauté with fresh mushrooms in 2 tablespoons butter, for about 15 minutes.

Purée mushrooms in a food processor or blender. Put purée in saucepan and add cream, salt, pepper, nutmeg and cayenne pepper. Simmer about 5 minutes to blend flavors. To serve, slice lamb and serve with wild mushroom sauce.

**Note:** *This sauce is also delicious with other roasted meats or chicken.*

# HERB MARINATED BUTTERFLIED LEG OF LAMB

SERVES 8 TO 10

*This is best prepared in summer when fresh herbs are plentiful.*

½  cup white wine vinegar

1  cup olive oil

2  tablespoons fresh thyme
    (or 2 teaspoons dried)

2  tablespoons fresh rosemary
    (or 2 teaspoons dried)

1  tablespoon fresh oregano
    (or 1 teaspoon dried)

½  cup firmly packed fresh mint
    (or 1 tablespoon dried)

2  large cloves garlic, peeled

1  teaspoon freshly ground pepper

5 to 6-pound butterflied leg of lamb
    pricked all over with the tip of a
    sharp knife

Fresh thyme and rosemary sprigs

In a blender or food processor blend vinegar, oil, herbs, garlic, and pepper until smooth and pour in a non-metallic dish slightly larger than the lamb. Add lamb and turn to coat both sides. Marinate in refrigerator, covered, for 24 hours.

Bring lamb to room temperature, discard marinade, and season with salt. Broil lamb under preheated broiler 4 inches from heat for 12 to 14 minutes each side for medium rare. Alternately the lamb may be grilled on a rack 5 to 6 inches over glowing coals for 10 to 12 minutes per side for medium rare.

Transfer the lamb to a carving board and let it stand for 10 minutes. Holding a sharp knife at a 45 degree angle, slice the lamb thinly across the grain. Arrange the lamb on a platter and garnish with fresh thyme and rosemary sprigs.

# GRILLED LAMB CHOPS WITH ANCHOVY BUTTER

SERVES 4

8   loin lamb chops, cut 1-inch thick
    and trimmed

**MARINADE**

2   tablespoons wine vinegar

1   tablespoon fresh lemon juice

2   teaspoons Dijon mustard

3   tablespoons olive oil

1   clove garlic, minced

¼   teaspoon ground ginger
    (or 1 teaspoon grated fresh ginger)

1   teaspoon rosemary

¼   teaspoon salt

1   small onion, sliced

**ANCHOVY BUTTER**

1   clove garlic, minced

1   tablespoon olive oil

½   cup (1 stick) butter, softened

1   teaspoon anchovy paste

4   anchovy fillets, minced

⅛   teaspoon superfine sugar

Salt and freshly ground pepper to taste

Place lamb chops in a deep ceramic or glass bowl. Combine marinade ingredients and pour over chops. Cover and marinate in the refrigerator for 4 to 5 hours. Grill over a hot charcoal fire or under an oven broiler for 5 minutes per side for medium rare.

**TO PREPARE THE ANCHOVY BUTTER,** sauté the garlic briefly in olive oil until fragrant. Set aside to cool. Combine the butter with the anchovy paste, anchovies, sugar, salt and pepper in a bowl. Add garlic and refrigerate until serving time. To serve place a dollop of herb butter on top of each grilled chop.

147

**Meats**

# LAMB POT PIE

*For a dinner party you might consider baking this in individual gratin dishes or large custard cups.*

¼ cup (½ stick) butter

2½ pounds boneless lamb,
    cut in 1-inch pieces

*Salt and freshly ground pepper to taste*

6 large tart apples, peeled,
    cored, and chopped

2 tablespoons brown sugar

½ teaspoon ground cinnamon

½ pound fresh mushrooms, sliced

2 large onions, thinly sliced

2 tablespoons butter

2 tablespoons flour

2 cups beef broth (homemade or canned)

1 tablespoon tomato paste

2 tablespoons dry vermouth

**PIE CRUST***

2½ cups sifted flour

¼ cup solid vegetable shortening

1 teaspoon salt

½ cup (1 stick) butter

2 to 5 tablespoons ice water

In a heavy skillet, heat butter and brown meat. Season with salt and pepper. Remove meat and drain on paper towels. Set skillet aside, reserving drippings.

In a greased 3-quart ovenproof casserole, place half the meat and cover with half the apples. Mix brown sugar and cinnamon. Sprinkle half on apples.

Next layer half the mushrooms and half the onions. Repeat layers of meat, apples, cinnamon mixture, mushrooms and onions.

Measure 2 tablespoons drippings reserved from meat and return to skillet. Add butter and heat until bubbly. Add flour and brown 3 to 4 minutes.

Stir in broth and bring to a boil. Reduce heat and simmer 15 minutes or until thick. Stir in tomato paste, salt, pepper and vermouth. Pour over lamb.

Preheat oven to 425° F.

**TO PREPARE PIE CRUST**, mix flour, shortening, salt and butter. Cut with a pastry blender until well mixed. Add water as needed to form a ball. Knead and roll out. Cover lamb with pastry and prick with a fork. Bake, covered with foil, for 10 minutes. Reduce heat to 350° F. and bake for 1 hour and 20 minutes.

**Note:** *This pie can be assembled hours in advance and baked just before serving.*

\* *A double top crust is especially tasty with this pie.
The extra crust nicely balances the hearty lamb chunks.
Apply one crust, brush with melted butter and prick.
Top with second crust and prick. (Be sure to double the
amount of pastry dough.)*

# LAMB AND EGGPLANT CURRY WITH PRUNES

SERVES 8

*An improvisational curry for heartland appetites.*

½   cup (1 stick) butter

2   tablespoons flour

¼   cup soy sauce

¼   cup honey

½   cup pure maple syrup

1   (14 to 16-ounce) can tomatoes,
    drained and chopped

1   cup red wine

1   teaspoon brandy

1   teaspoon Dijon mustard

½   teaspoon nutmeg

½   teaspoon cinnamon

1 to 2 tablespoons curry powder
    (or more to taste)

3 to 4 tablespoons vegetable oil

3   pounds lean, boneless lamb, cut into
    ½-inch cubes

1   medium red onion, diced medium fine
    (½ cup)

1   large eggplant, peeled and cut into
    ½-inch cubes

2   ounces pitted prunes

In a large pot, melt butter over low heat and whisk in the flour. Cook, whisking constantly, for 2 minutes. Add soy sauce, honey, syrup, tomatoes, wine, brandy, mustard, nutmeg, cinnamon and curry. Blend and simmer 15 to 20 minutes, stirring occasionally.

Meanwhile, in another large pan, heat the oil and sauté lamb and onion, until lamb is cooked, about 10 minutes for medium rare. Toss in eggplant and prunes and add curry sauce. Heat through and simmer 6 to 8 minutes, or until eggplant is tender and cooked through. Serve over rice.

149

**Meats**

# PORK ROAST WITH CIDER GRAVY

*The pepper mustard topping forms a delicious crisp crust.*

¼ cup (½ stick) plus 1 tablespoon
   unsalted butter, room temperature

4½-pound boneless pork loin roast,
   rolled and tied

2 tablespoons flour

2 tablespoons Dijon mustard

1 tablespoon dry mustard

3 tablespoons cracked black peppercorns

1 tablespoon whole mustard seeds

2 teaspoons light brown sugar

2 teaspoons dried thyme, crumbled

150

### GRAVY

1½ cups apple cider

3 tablespoons apple brandy

2 tablespoons flour

¾ cup chicken broth (homemade or canned)

1 tablespoon cider vinegar

1 teaspoon Dijon mustard

*Salt and freshly ground pepper to taste*

Preheat oven to 475° F. Melt 1 tablespoon butter in heavy large skillet over medium-high heat. Add roast and cook until brown, about 4 minutes per side. Transfer to roasting pan.

Combine remaining ¼ cup butter with flour, mustards, peppercorns, mustard seeds, sugar and thyme in bowl. Spread paste over top and sides of roast. Roast 30 minutes.

Reduce heat to 325° F. Continue cooking about 1½ hours until done. Remove from pan, place on a warm platter and tent with foil. Drain and reserve drippings.

**TO PREPARE GRAVY**, heat roasting pan over medium-low heat. Add cider and boil until liquid is reduced to ¾ cup, stirring to blend browned particles. Stir in apple brandy and boil 1 minute.

Heat 2 tablespoons of the reserved drippings in saucepan over medium-high heat. Add flour and stir until golden brown, about 2 minutes. Whisk in cider mixture and broth. Simmer until thickened, stirring occasionally, about 2 minutes.

Remove from heat. Mix in cider vinegar and mustard. Season with salt and pepper. Carve roast and serve with gravy.

# BRAISED PORK CHOPS WITH WILD MUSHROOMS

SERVES 4

*An elegant Italian recipe that dresses up the everyday pork chop.*

1 ounce dried, imported wild mushrooms (available at specialty food stores)

6 tablespoons vegetable oil, divided

2 pounds center cut loin pork chops, ½-inch thick

½ cup dry white wine

½ cup canned Italian plum tomatoes, drained

½ cup heavy cream

Salt and freshly ground pepper to taste

½ pound fresh mushrooms

Soak the dried mushrooms for at least 30 minutes in 2 cups of warm water. Lift mushrooms out of water, rinse and pat dry. Cut up in large pieces and set aside. Filter mushroom water (a paper coffee filter works well) and reserve.

Heat 3 tablespoons of vegetable oil in a sauté pan large enough to accommodate the chops in a single layer. When the oil is hot, place chops in pan and brown them well over medium high heat. Add white wine and let it bubble for a few minutes.

Add tomatoes, cream, salt and pepper and reconstituted wild mushrooms. Turn heat to medium low and cover the pan. Cook 45 minutes to 1 hour, turning from time to time.

While chops cook, boil mushroom water to reduce it to ⅓ cup. Wash and slice fresh mushrooms and sauté them in remaining 3 tablespoons of oil. Sprinkle with salt and pepper and add reduced mushroom liquid to pan. Remove from heat when liquid has evaporated.

When pork chops are tender, add mushrooms, turn chops and stir mushrooms in the sauce. Cook for another 5 to 8 minutes at medium low heat. Serve immediately. ▨

*151*

**Meats**

# PORK CHOPS WITH GRUYÈRE

SERVES 4

*Pork chops are especially flavorful in this unusual recipe.*

4   loin pork chops, about 1½-inches thick

*Salt and freshly ground pepper to taste*

1   tablespoon vegetable oil

¼   pound grated Gruyère cheese

1   tablespoon Dijon mustard

1   tablespoon heavy cream

1   teaspoon minced garlic

1   tablespoon finely chopped chives

1   egg yolk

2   tablespoons dry white wine

2   tablespoons water

Sprinkle chops with salt and pepper. Heat oil and brown chops in heavy skillet on both sides until cooked through but not dry, about 8 to 10 minutes per side.

Preheat broiler. As chops cook, blend cheese, mustard, cream, garlic, chives and egg yolk. When chops are cooked remove from skillet. Place about 1 tablespoon of cheese mixture on one side of chop and smooth to cover. Cook chops under broiler until top is browned. Remove chops to warm platter.

Add wine and water to skillet stirring to loosen particles. Bring to boil and stir to dissolve particles that cling to bottom and sides of the skillet. Pour sauce over the chops and serve. 🕸

# KENTUCKY TENDERLOINS

SERVES 4 TO 6 DEPENDING ON SIZE OF TENDERLOINS

2   pork tenderloins

½   cup soy sauce

½   cup bourbon

1   tablespoon brown sugar

*Caraway seeds to taste*

*Freshly ground pepper to taste*

1   medium onion, sliced

4   strips bacon

1   cup sour cream

1   teaspoon dried dill
    (or 1 tablespoon fresh, minced)

Place pork tenderloins in a glass dish. Blend soy sauce, bourbon and brown sugar to make a marinade and pour over meat. Refrigerate, covered, for at least 2 hours.

Before baking, sprinkle tenderloins with caraway seeds and black pepper and top with onion and bacon strips. Bake in preheated 300° F. oven about 1½ hours until done, basting occasionally. Slice and pass with a bowl of sour cream sprinkled with dill. 🕸

152

# PORK TENDERLOIN (a favorite from the original *Artist in the Kitchen*)

*This oven-barbecued pork tenderloin is a do-ahead family favorite.*

2   small pork tenderloins

1   clove garlic, halved

1   teaspoon garlic salt

Salt and freshly ground pepper to taste

½   cup plus 2½ tablespoons dark corn syrup

½   cup ketchup

1   cup water

3   tablespoons soy sauce

Potatoes, carrots, onions (optional)

Preheat oven to 325° F. Rub tenderloins with cut clove of garlic, and sprinkle with garlic salt; salt and pepper generously. Place in open baking dish and cover tops with 2½ tablespoons syrup to seal in the seasonings and glaze the meat.

Mix remaining corn syrup, ketchup, water and soy sauce and pour into dish around tenderloins. Bake uncovered for 2½ to 3 hours.

Peeled potatoes, carrots and onions may be added and cooked for about 2 hours. Baste meat and vegetables every half hour with sauce. Make more sauce if needed.

To serve, slice meat thinly and strain sauce into gravy dish. If sauce is too thick, add a little warm water.

**Note:** *Serve as a meat course or on small rolls for a buffet.*

153

**Meats**

# SECOND MARRIAGE PORK WITH BARBECUE SAUCE

SERVES 4 TO 6

*The antidote to gray February skies and lingering winter chill. A versatile and easy dish that will make you plan ahead for leftovers.*

2 to 3 pounds boneless cooked pork, cut into 2-inch chunks

3 cloves garlic, minced

¼ cup cider vinegar

4 cups water

2 teaspoons salt

## SAUCE

1 medium onion, finely chopped (½ cup)

2 tablespoons oil

3 tablespoons cider vinegar

2 teaspoons salt

¾ cup ketchup

3 tablespoons light brown sugar

2 tablespoons Worcestershire sauce

1 tablespoon dried mustard

2 teaspoons Tabasco

1 teaspoon freshly ground black pepper

2 tablespoons soy sauce

⅛ teaspoon cayenne

1 teaspoon ground cumin

In a large non-metallic saucepan, add pork chunks, garlic, vinegar and water. Bring to a boil and then reduce heat to simmer, partially covered, for 1 to 1½ hours. Meat will be very tender.

Remove chunks with slotted spoon and, when cool enough to handle, shred the pork coarsely. Discard cooking liquid.

TO PREPARE THE SAUCE, sauté the onion in 2 tablespoons oil in a small saucepan for about 5 minutes. Add remaining ingredients and whisk over low heat for 2 to 3 minutes, until sugar dissolves.

Return pork to large pan, stir in barbecue sauce and heat until sauce thickens, about 20 minutes. Serve with rice, on a bun or over onion and garlic mashed potatoes (see page 90).

**Note:** *May be prepared ahead and reheated.*

# CORNICHON PORK PATTIES

*Children and parents will like these crispy alternatives to traditional "burgers."*

2   tablespoons butter, divided

2   medium onions, finely chopped (1 cup)

½   teaspoon minced garlic

1½  pounds lean ground pork

½   cup finely chopped cornichons
    (small imported pickles)

¼   teaspoon ground cumin

2   tablespoons Dijon mustard

1   egg, lightly beaten

1   cup fine, fresh bread crumbs, divided

1   cup chicken broth
    (homemade or canned), divided

Salt and freshly ground pepper to taste

¼   cup vegetable oil

2   tablespoons red wine vinegar

1   teaspoon tomato paste

Heat 1 tablespoon butter in small skillet, add onions and garlic. Cook until soft. Cool briefly and add to pork. Add chopped cornichons. Add cumin, mustard, egg, ½ cup bread crumbs, ¼ cup broth, salt and pepper.

Blend with fingers. Shape into 8 patties. Coat patties with remaining bread crumbs. Heat oil in 1 or 2 skillets. Cook 4 to 5 minutes, turn carefully and cook about 8 more minutes. Transfer to warm platter.

Pour off fat from skillet, add vinegar, stirring to loosen browned particles. Cook briefly, add remaining broth and tomato paste. Cook until reduced to ½ cup. Swirl in remaining tablespoon of butter and pour over patties. 

155

**Meats**

# COGNAC VEAL ROAST

SERVES 6

½ cup (1 stick) unsalted butter,
   at room temperature

2 shallots, chopped

1½ tablespoons chopped fresh parsley

1 teaspoon thyme

3 tablespoons Cognac or Calvados, divided

2½ teaspoons Dijon mustard

1 teaspoon salt, divided

1 teaspoon freshly ground pepper, divided

3-pound veal loin or shoulder roast,
   rolled and tied

¼ cup dry white wine

Combine the butter, shallots, parsley, thyme, 1½ tablespoons of Cognac, mustard, ½ teaspoon salt and ½ teaspoon pepper in a food processor or a bowl and blend well. Shape this mixture into a long cylinder, wrap it in plastic, and refrigerate for at least 1 hour. When butter is firm, cut it into 10 pieces.

Make 10 long, thin cuts in the veal roast at equal intervals. Insert a piece of butter into each cut. Wrap the roast in plastic wrap and refrigerate until the butter firms up again, about 2 hours. (The roast can be prepared to this point up to a day in advance. Remove the meat from the refrigerator about 30 minutes before roasting.)

Preheat oven to 450° F. Unwrap the meat, place it in a small roasting pan and roast for 10 minutes. Reduce the oven temperature to 325° F. and pour the wine into the bottom of the pan. Continue to roast the meat until the internal temperature reaches 145 to 150° F., about 1 hour and 20 minutes. Remove roast to a warm serving platter and tent with foil.

Pour off any grease from the roasting pan and place the pan over high heat. When the pan begins to smoke, add 1 cup of water and stir, scraping up the browned particles from the bottom of the pan. Stir in remaining 1½ tablespoons of Cognac and boil, stirring, until pan juices are reduced to about ½ cup, about 3 minutes. Season the sauce with the remaining ½ teaspoon each of salt and pepper.

Carve the roast into ¼-inch-thick slices and pour any accumulated juices into the sauce. Serve at once with the sauce on the side.

**Note:** *The butter mixture may be prepared up to a week in advance and frozen.*

# STUFFED VEAL CHOPS

SERVES 4

*A luxurious stuffing enhances the simple veal chop.*

¾  ounce dried Porcini mushrooms*

1  cup warm water

1  teaspoon butter

3  tablespoons olive oil, divided

2  scallions, chopped

⅛  teaspoon salt

⅛  teaspoon freshly ground pepper

⅓  pound thinly sliced prosciutto,
    finely chopped

4  veal rib or loin chops
    (about ¾ pound each)

1  cup dry white wine

Salt and freshly ground pepper to taste

Place mushrooms in small bowl. Add warm water and soak 30 minutes. Remove mushrooms from liquid with a slotted spoon and rinse thoroughly. Filter mushroom liquid (a paper coffee filter works well) and reserve. Chop mushrooms.

Melt butter with 1 tablespoon oil in heavy large skillet over medium heat. Add onions and sauté 2 minutes. Add mushrooms, 1½ tablespoons reserved mushroom liquid, salt and pepper. Cover and cook 2 minutes. Remove from heat. Mix in prosciutto.

Preheat oven to 350° F.

Starting at center of side opposite bone of veal chop, cut 1-inch-long, 1-inch-deep slit. Make a pocket, being careful not to cut through meat. Repeat cutting procedure with remaining chops. Spoon stuffing into pockets. Skewer closed with toothpicks if necessary.

Heat 2 tablespoons oil in an ovenproof pan over high heat. Add chops and brown well, about 1 minute per side. Reduce heat to medium and cook 3 minutes per side. Transfer pan to oven and cook chops to desired degree of doneness, 15 minutes for medium. Transfer chops to plates. Tent with foil to keep warm.

Pour off all but 1 tablespoon oil from skillet. Place pan over medium heat. Add wine and remaining mushroom liquid and bring to a boil, scraping up any browned bits. Boil until liquid is reduced to ½ cup, about 5 minutes. Season with salt and pepper. Pour over chops and serve.

**Note:** *Stuffing can be prepared 1 day ahead and refrigerated. Bring to room temperature before inserting in veal.*

* *Available at specialty food stores.*

# VEAL SCALLOPS WITH ARTICHOKES

(a favorite from the original *Artist in the Kitchen*)

SERVES 6

18 *thin veal scallops, about 2 ounces each*

*Flour for dredging*

2   *cups artichoke hearts, sliced*

½   *cup (1 stick) butter*

¾   *cup dry white wine*

2   *cups heavy cream*

¾   *cup veal or beef broth
      (homemade or canned)*

*Salt and freshly ground pepper to taste*

Lightly flour the scallops and quickly sauté them with the artichokes in butter. Remove to a warm platter.

Pour off butter, add wine and reduce to half. Add cream, broth and seasonings. Reduce cream and broth to half, then pour over scallops and artichokes. Serve with risotto or buttered pasta. ▣

# LEMON VEAL

SERVES 6

2   *pounds veal scallops
      (pounded until very thin)*

*Flour, salt and white pepper for dredging*

4   *tablespoons (½ stick) butter, divided*

2   *tablespoons olive oil*

¼   *cup fresh lemon juice*

1½ *cups dry white wine*

½   *pound fresh mushrooms, sliced*

1   *tablespoon arrowroot or cornstarch*

3   *tablespoons cold water*

2   *lemons, sliced*

*Salt and white pepper to taste*

Preheat oven to 250° F. Lightly dust veal with salt, pepper and flour. In a hot skillet add 2 tablespoons butter and oil and when sizzling sauté veal, about 2 minutes per side. Remove to a warm platter.

Add remaining butter to skillet and sauté mushrooms for 10 minutes. Remove mushrooms and put on top of veal; keep platter warm in oven.

Add lemon juice to butter in skillet, increase heat and add wine. Bring liquid almost to a boil, stirring. Dissolve arrowroot in cold water and add to butter and wine mixture, stirring constantly while it thickens. When smooth, add lemon slices. Pour over veal and mushrooms. ▣

# VEAL STEW

*This is a delicious and versatile stew. Use pork as a tasty, economical substitute for the veal.*

8   small dried morel mushrooms

3   cups chicken broth
    (homemade or canned), divided

¼   cup peanut oil, divided

1   large red onion, chopped (1 cup)

3   leeks, trimmed, well-washed and sliced

12  shallots, minced

3   cloves garlic, minced

16  sage leaves, divided

½   pound fresh mushrooms, sliced

3   pounds boneless veal,
    cut into 1-inch pieces

Salt and freshly ground pepper to taste

½   cup flour

½   cup port wine

Preheat oven to 325° F. Soak dried mushrooms in 1 cup of warm chicken broth for 20 minutes. Heat half the oil in a large sauté pan; sauté the onions, leeks, shallots and garlic over medium-low heat until tender and translucent.

While the onions are cooking, remove the softened mushrooms from the broth with a slotted spoon. Strain the broth (a paper coffee filter works well) and reserve. Rinse the mushrooms to remove any sand or grit and pat dry. Chop 5 sage leaves and add them and the mushrooms to the cooked onions. Cook another 2 minutes, then transfer everything to a heavy ovenproof casserole. Using the same pan, heat the remaining oil. Sauté the fresh mushrooms a few minutes. Remove with a slotted spoon to the casserole.

Season, flour and brown the meat over medium-high heat (do not crowd the meat or it will not brown). Remove the browned veal to the casserole with the mushrooms.

Deglaze the pan with port, add the mushroom-infused chicken broth and remaining chicken broth. Bring to a boil and reduce by ⅓. Pour over the veal, mushrooms and onions. Place in the oven, cover and cook about 45 minutes or until the meat is tender. Serve garnished with remaining sage leaves. 🔲

**Note:** *If using pork shoulder, increase cooking time to about 1½ hours.*

# SATÉ (INDONESIAN KEBABS)

*These kebabs are delicious! The mixing technique for the marinade is unorthodox, but wonderfully efficient and mess-free.*

3   tablespoons creamy peanut butter

2   tablespoons soy sauce

2   tablespoons ground coriander

1   tablespoon ground cumin

1   clove garlic, minced

½   teaspoon crushed red pepper flakes

2   pounds of pork tenderloin, chicken breast or beef sirloin, cut in 1-inch cubes

## DIPPING SAUCE

2   tablespoons creamy peanut butter

½   cup soy sauce

1   tablespoon molasses

1   tablespoon crushed red pepper flakes

1   clove garlic, minced

Fresh mint leaves

Combine peanut butter, soy sauce and spices in a large resealable plastic freezer/storage bag and mash together until blended. Add meat to bag and blend with spices. Marinate for 1 to 5 hours.

Thread the meat on skewers.* Grill over charcoal or broil 4 inches from heat about 3 minutes per side. Do not overcook.

TO PREPARE DIPPING SAUCE, combine all ingredients in food processor or blender and let stand 1 hour before serving.

To serve, drizzle dipping sauce over meat or serve sauce in individual bowls. Garnish satés with fresh mint and serve with rice.

* If using bamboo skewers, first soak them in cold water for ½ hour to keep them from burning.

# Sun Valley Brunch

SERVES 12

*This homey casserole is perfect for a pre-game meal.*

6   tablespoons (¾ stick) unsalted butter

⅓   cup flour

3   cups milk

3   eggs, lightly beaten

3   cups grated sharp Cheddar or
    Swiss cheese (about ¾ pound)

2   tablespoons Dijon mustard

½   teaspoon freshly grated nutmeg

⅓   teaspoon freshly ground pepper

2   pounds boiling potatoes,
    sliced ¼-inch thick

3   tablespoons olive oil

2   large onions, thinly sliced

1   cup Madeira

1   (10-ounce) package frozen chopped
    spinach, thawed and squeezed dry

1½  pounds thinly sliced baked ham

½   cup freshly grated Parmesan cheese

In medium saucepan, melt butter over low heat. Add flour and cook, stirring constantly for 2 to 3 minutes without letting it brown. Gradually whisk in milk until smooth. Bring to a boil over moderate heat, whisking constantly. Reduce heat to low and simmer for 10 minutes, whisking occasionally. Remove from heat.

Blend in a few tablespoons of the warm sauce into the beaten eggs and then whisk eggs into cream sauce. Stir in Cheddar or Swiss cheese, mustard, nutmeg and pepper until blended. Press a piece of plastic wrap directly onto surface of cheese sauce.

In a large saucepan of boiling salted water, cook potatoes until tender, 12 to 15 minutes. Drain and pat dry. Meanwhile, heat olive oil in a large skillet. Add onions and cook over low heat, stirring occasionally, until softened but not browned, about 10 minutes.

Add Madeira, increase heat to high and boil 7 to 10 minutes until liquid is reduced to about 2 tablespoons. Stir in spinach and set aside.

Preheat oven to 350° F. Lightly butter a shallow 3-quart baking dish. Layer ⅓ of ham slices evenly over bottom of dish. Top with ½ of cooked potatoes and spread ⅓ of cheese sauce evenly over top. Cover with all onion and spinach mixture. Repeat layering with ½ of remaining ham, all remaining potatoes and ½ of remaining cheese sauce. Top with remaining ham and cheese sauce and sprinkle Parmesan cheese evenly over top.

Bake for 30 minutes, or until heated through. To brown top, broil about 4 inches from heat until browned and bubbly, 2 to 3 minutes. Let cool for 10 minutes before serving. ▩

# RICE & PASTA

Detail from an embroidered bed valance

made in Italy in the 16th century.

A tradition of domestic embroideries existed

in the Mediterranean for centuries.

# ASPARAGUS RICE ORIENTAL

SERVES 4

1   pound fresh asparagus, trimmed

3   tablespoons vegetable oil

1   clove garlic, minced

¼   teaspoon grated fresh ginger

2   cups chicken broth
    (homemade or canned)

¼   cup chopped scallions

2   teaspoons soy sauce

½   teaspoon sugar

1   cup rice

Cut asparagus diagonally into 2-inch lengths, keeping bottom ends separate.

Heat oil in wok or Dutch oven. Add garlic, ginger and asparagus bottoms. Stir-fry 1 minute.

Add remaining asparagus and stir-fry 2 minutes. Remove asparagus and set aside.

Add broth, scallions, soy sauce and sugar. Bring to a boil, stir in rice. Cover, reduce heat to low and simmer 15 minutes. Add asparagus and cook 5 more minutes.

# SAFFRON RICE WITH VEGETABLES

SERVES 6

*This colorful and healthy rice dish is a fine complement to grilled chicken or fish.*

4    cups chicken broth
     (homemade or canned)

1    tablespoon olive oil

1    medium onion, finely chopped (½ cup)

4    large cloves garlic, minced

1½  cups rice

1    green bell pepper, cut into ¼-inch strips

1    red bell pepper, cut into ¼-inch strips

3    tomatoes, peeled, seeded and chopped

¼    cup dry white wine

¼    teaspoon saffron threads

1    cup fresh shelled or frozen tiny peas

Salt and freshly ground pepper to taste

Bring chicken broth to a simmer in a saucepan. Meanwhile, heat the oil in a skillet and add onion and garlic. Cook, stirring, until onion is tender.

Add rice and cook until rice is coated with oil, about 1 minute. Stir in peppers and tomatoes and cook together for 1 or 2 minutes.

Add wine and continue to cook, stirring until liquid is absorbed. Add simmering chicken broth and saffron. Bring to a slow boil over medium heat and cook for 25 minutes, uncovered.

Add peas and continue cooking until all liquid is absorbed or until rice is al dente, about 10 minutes. Pour off any remaining broth, season with salt and pepper to taste and serve.

# RIS SAUVAGE

*Wild rice has never tasted so good. An excellent party dish.*

½   *pound wild rice (about 1 cup)*

2   *quarts boiling water*

1   *tablespoon salt*

¼   *cup cognac*

½   *cup currants*

1   *small onion, chopped (¼ cup)*

¼   *cup (½ stick) butter, divided*

1   *cup beef broth (homemade or canned)*

¼   *cup chopped shallots*

½   *cup pine nuts*

*Salt and freshly ground pepper to taste*

¼   *cup chopped fresh parsley*

Preheat oven to 350° F. Drop rice into boiling water with salt. Cook uncovered 5 minutes. Drain and set aside. Meanwhile, pour cognac over currants and soak about 20 minutes.

In a heavy casserole, sauté onion in 2 tablespoons butter until soft. Add rice and stir to allow rice to absorb butter. Add broth. Cover and place in oven for about 30 minutes. Add currants with cognac and cook another 5 to 15 minutes, until rice is tender and broth is absorbed. If rice is dry and too firm, add a little warm water and continue cooking until tender.

Sauté shallots in remaining butter until limp and just starting to brown. Stir into cooked rice. Add pine nuts, salt, pepper and parsley.

**Note:** *This dish can be made ahead and gently reheated. Add additional broth or water if necessary.*

# SAVORY RICE

SERVES 4

1   medium onion, chopped (½ cup)

3   tablespoons olive oil (or less)

½   cup diced celery

¼   cup diced red bell pepper

1   cup brown rice
    (or ¾ cup brown and ¼ cup wild)

3   cups chicken broth
    (homemade or canned)

½   teaspoon salt

Pepper to taste

1   teaspoon fresh sage leaves, minced
    (or ¼ teaspoon dried)

½   cup sliced fresh mushrooms

2   tablespoons chopped fresh parsley

Sauté onion in oil until golden but not browned. Add celery and pepper, raise heat and sauté 2 minutes. Stir in rice for 2 minutes more so that rice absorbs some of oil.

Add broth, salt, pepper, sage and mushrooms. Cover and simmer about 1 hour.

When rice is tender and broth is absorbed, stir in fresh parsley.

# BASIC RISOTTO

SERVES 6

4   cups chicken, beef or vegetable broth
    (homemade or canned)

1   small onion, chopped (¼ cup)

¼   cup (½ stick) butter, divided

3   tablespoons olive oil

2   cups Arborio rice*

1   cup freshly grated Parmesan cheese

**Optional additions:** 1 cup cooked crabmeat, cooked shredded chicken, minced ham or sautéed fresh spinach or zucchini.

Heat broth until it simmers and set aside. In a heavy-bottomed skillet or pot (not aluminum or copper), sauté onion in 2 tablespoons butter and oil. Do not let the onion brown. Add rice and stir until it is coated with butter/oil mixture and looks translucent.

Begin adding broth, ½ cup at a time, stirring constantly and allowing broth to be fully absorbed before adding more. Temperature of the dish must remain constant to prevent stickiness. Continue until rice is tender (about 18 minutes from when broth is first added). If you run out of broth before rice is tender, add water.

When rice is tender, swirl in rest of the butter, any additions desired, and Parmesan cheese. Serve immediately as a first course or as a light dinner with salad.

* Available at specialty food stores.

# RISOTTO WITH PORCINI MUSHROOMS

SERVES 6

1   ounce dried Porcini mushrooms*

2   cups chicken, beef or vegetable broth
    (homemade or canned)

1   small onion, chopped (¼ cup)

4   tablespoons (½ stick) butter, divided

3   tablespoons olive oil

2   cups Arborio rice*

1   cup freshly grated Parmesan cheese

Soak mushrooms in 2 cups hot water for about
30 minutes. Lift them out of water with a slotted spoon,
reserving the liquid. Rinse mushrooms thoroughly until
they are free of grit or sand. Chop coarsely and set aside.

Strain liquid through a sieve lined with paper towels
or a coffee filter and reserve. Heat broth until it simmers
and set aside.

In a heavy-bottomed skillet or pot (not aluminum or
copper), sauté onion in 2 tablespoons butter and oil.
Do not let the onion brown. Add rice and stir until
coated with butter-oil mixture and looks translucent.

Begin adding broth, ½ cup at a time, stirring constantly
and allowing the broth to be fully absorbed before
adding more. Add chopped mushrooms and reserved
mushroom liquid, ½ cup at a time, until rice has
absorbed it all. Temperature of the dish must remain
constant to prevent stickiness. Continue until rice is
tender (about 18 minutes from when broth is first
added). If you run out of broth before rice is tender,
add water.

When rice is tender, swirl in rest of butter and Parmesan
cheese. Serve immediately as a first course or light
dinner with salad. ✤

* Available at specialty food stores.

# BARLEY AND SUMMER VEGETABLE CASSEROLE

SERVES 6

½   cup brown rice

½   cup pearl barley

3   cups sliced zucchini

⅔   cup chopped onion

1   green or yellow bell pepper,
    cut in ½-inch strips

⅓   cup tomato paste

1   clove garlic, minced

1   teaspoon dried basil or oregano

½   teaspoon sugar

*Salt and freshly ground pepper to taste*

1   large tomato, sliced

¾   cup shredded part-skim Mozzarella
    or Cheddar cheese

Rinse rice and barley under cold running water.
Bring 2½ cups of water to boil in a saucepan and stir
in rice and barley. Cover and reduce heat; simmer for
40 minutes or until water is absorbed and rice is tender.

Preheat oven to 325° F. Grease an 11 x 7-inch baking
dish and spread rice mixture in bottom.

In saucepan with small amount of boiling water, cook
zucchini, onion and pepper for 2 to 3 minutes or until
crisp-tender and drain. Spread over rice mixture.

In small bowl combine ⅔ cups water, tomato paste,
garlic, basil, sugar, salt and pepper. Pour over vegetables.
Arrange tomato slices on top.

Cover and bake for 25 minutes or until heated through.
Sprinkle with cheese and bake, uncovered, for
5 minutes longer or until cheese melts.

# ORZO WITH PINE NUTS AND SUN-DRIED TOMATOES

SERVES 3 TO 4

1½ tablespoons olive oil

3 tablespoons pine nuts

¼ cup oil-packed sun-dried tomatoes, drained and chopped

Salt and freshly ground pepper to taste

½ pound orzo (a small rice-sized pasta sometimes called Rosa Marina)

Freshly grated Parmesan cheese to taste (optional)

Heat oil in small heavy saucepan over medium heat. When oil is hot, add pine nuts and sun-dried tomatoes and sauté 2 to 3 minutes, until nuts are lightly golden and tomatoes are heated through. Turn off heat and season with salt and pepper to taste. Set aside.

Cook orzo for 8 to 10 minutes until tender but firm. Drain. Place orzo in a large bowl and pour sauce over the pasta. Toss well and sprinkle with cheese if desired.

# ORZO WITH DILLED LEMON SAUCE

SERVES 6 TO 8

*A delicious accompaniment to grilled fish, meat, or poultry.*

3 tablespoons fresh lemon juice, or to taste

3 teaspoons Dijon mustard

5 scallions, chopped, including crisp green ends

3 tablespoons snipped fresh dill (or 1 tablespoon dried) plus additional for garnish

Salt and freshly ground pepper to taste

1 cup chicken broth (homemade or canned)

¼ cup olive oil

1 pound orzo (a small rice-sized pasta sometimes called Rosa Marina), cooked and drained

2 (14-ounce) cans artichoke hearts, drained, rinsed and quartered

1 cup Kalamata or other brine-cured olives, pitted, halved and patted dry on paper towels

¼ pound Feta cheese, crumbled

Heat broth. In food processor or blender combine lemon juice, mustard, scallions, dill, salt and pepper. With motor running, add heated broth and then the oil in a stream and blend well.

In a large bowl toss orzo with sauce, stir in artichokes, olives and Feta. Garnish dish with additional fresh dill. Serve at room temperature on lettuce leaves.

# COUSCOUS WITH RAISINS

⅓ cup raisins

1 tablespoon olive oil

1 small onion, chopped (¼ cup)

1 teaspoon minced garlic

1½ cups boiling water

⅛ teaspoon ground cinnamon

⅛ teaspoon ground cumin

Salt and freshly ground pepper to taste

1 cup quick-cooking couscous

1 teaspoon finely chopped fresh mint

1 tablespoon fresh lemon juice

1 teaspoon balsamic vinegar

Toasted almonds or pine nuts (optional)

Place raisins in a small bowl and cover with lukewarm water. Soak about 15 minutes and drain.

While raisins are soaking, heat oil in a saucepan over low heat and add onion and garlic and cook, stirring until soft. Do not brown. Add water, raisins, cinnamon, cumin, salt and pepper and bring to a boil.

Remove from heat and add couscous. Add mint, lemon juice and vinegar. Cover and let stand 5 minutes.

Uncover and fluff couscous with a fork. Add almonds or pine nuts if desired. ❧

**Note:** *For a delicious alternative, substitute chopped dried apricots for the raisins in this fragrant dish.*

# EGGPLANT COUSCOUS

SERVES 4

*Couscous is so versatile and easy, here keeping company with some pungent spices.*

2 tablespoons olive oil

2 shallots, finely chopped

1 small onion, finely chopped (¼ cup)

¼ teaspoon cumin

¼ teaspoon ground coriander

1 small eggplant cut into ¼-inch cubes

Salt and freshly ground pepper to taste

1 cup quick-cooking couscous

1 tablespoon butter

1 tablespoon fresh lemon juice

Heat oil in a heavy-bottomed skillet. Add shallots, onions, cumin, coriander, eggplant, salt and pepper. Cook over medium-high heat, stirring, until soft but not brown.

Add 1 cup of water and bring to a boil. Add couscous and blend well. Cover tightly, remove from heat and let stand 5 minutes.

Add butter and lemon juice and blend with a fork. Keep warm. ❧

# BAKED STUFFED CURLY LASAGNA

SERVES 10

*An exceptionally stylish presentation for a traditional favorite.*

15 or 16 curly lasagna noodles

2 (10-ounce) packages frozen spinach, thawed and squeezed dry

¼ cup minced fresh parsley

2 cups freshly grated Parmesan cheese, divided

2 (15-ounce) cartons ricotta cheese

*Salt and freshly ground pepper to taste*

½ teaspoon grated nutmeg

3 to 4 tablespoons vegetable oil

2 cloves garlic, minced

2 medium onions, chopped (1 cup)

5 cups tomato sauce

2 teaspoons sugar

½ teaspoon dried basil

½ teaspoon dried oregano

Preheat oven to 350° F. Grease a large 2½-inch deep casserole. Cook noodles until tender but firm. Rinse in cold water, pat dry and cover until used.

Mix spinach with parsley, 1½ cups Parmesan, ricotta, salt, pepper and nutmeg. Spread about ⅓ cup of mixture onto each noodle. Roll up lengthwise and stand on end in casserole. Repeat with remaining noodles, using all cheese mixture.

Heat oil in heavy skillet or saucepan. Add garlic and onions and 1 cup water. Bring to a boil and simmer uncovered until water has cooked away and onion is soft and transparent. Add tomato sauce, sugar, basil, oregano, salt and pepper. Simmer 5 minutes, uncovered.

Pour over noodles. Cover and bake for about 30 minutes. Sprinkle with remaining Parmesan cheese before serving.

# ORIENTAL PASTA WITH GRILLED CHICKEN BREASTS

SERVES 4

2 whole boneless chicken breasts, skinned, washed and patted dry

## MARINADE

1 large clove garlic, minced

Grated peel and juice of ½ lemon

⅓ cup light soy sauce or dry white wine or combination

1 tablespoon vegetable oil

## PASTA

¼ cup sesame seeds

1 pound pasta (spaghetti or linguine is best)

1 bunch scallions, sliced

¼ teaspoon crushed red pepper flakes

## SAUCE

¼ cup peanut butter

¾ cup soy sauce (light or dark)

⅔ cup vegetable oil

2 tablespoons sugar

1 tablespoon grated fresh ginger

2 tablespoons white vinegar

½ cup julienned carrots

Combine marinade ingredients. Pour over chicken breasts in a non-aluminum pan or bowl and refrigerate for 1 to 2 hours.

Grill or broil about 5 to 6 minutes on each side or until completely done, basting with marinade. Slice into bite-sized pieces and set aside.

Toast sesame seeds by stirring them in a dry skillet over medium heat until they brown and pop. Set aside.

Cook pasta until tender but firm and drain. Combine with sesame seeds, scallions, chicken and red pepper.

**TO PREPARE SAUCE**, combine peanut butter, soy sauce, oil, sugar, ginger, vinegar and carrots in a saucepan. Heat only until peanut butter is melted and all ingredients combined. Combine sauce with pasta and serve hot or at room temperature.

172

# PENNE WITH SHRIMP

SERVES 2 (GENEROUSLY)

2  tablespoons olive oil

5  large cloves garlic, minced

1  red bell pepper, diced

½  pound shrimp, peeled, deveined, rinsed and patted dry

¾  teaspoon salt

Freshly ground pepper to taste

¼  teaspoon crushed red pepper flakes

6  ounces penne or other tubular pasta

1  cup frozen tiny peas
   (or 1 cup frozen sugar snaps)

12  small fresh basil leaves, minced
    (or 1 teaspoon dried)

3  tablespoons minced fresh parsley

½  cup diced fresh plum tomatoes,
   juiced, peeled and seeded

Heat oil in heavy skillet and sauté garlic over medium heat until garlic is just golden. Add red bell pepper and cook, stirring, about 2 minutes. Add shrimp and cook until opaque, about 2 to 3 minutes. Season with salt, pepper and pepper flakes. Set aside.

Cook pasta until almost tender, drop peas or sugar snaps into the pasta pot. Cook an additional 30 seconds; drain. Add peas and pasta to shrimp.

Gently stir in basil, parsley and tomato and correct seasoning. If pasta seems dry, add a little more olive oil. Serve immediately.

# PENNE WITH TOMATOES AND PORCINI

SERVES 4 TO 6

1  ounce dried Porcini mushrooms*

2  tablespoons finely chopped shallots

3  tablespoons olive oil

2  slices of pancetta (Italian bacon)
   or prosciutto, chopped
   (about 2 tablespoons)

1½  cups canned Italian tomatoes,
    cut up, with their juice

¼  teaspoon salt

Freshly ground pepper to taste

1  pound penne or other tubular noodle

Freshly grated Parmesan cheese

Soak mushrooms in 2 cups hot water for at least 30 minutes. Lift out of water with a slotted spoon, reserving liquid. Wash mushrooms thoroughly under running water until free of any grit; chop coarsely and set aside. Filter soaking liquid through a strainer lined with white paper towels or a coffee filter and reserve.

Sauté shallots in oil over medium heat until golden. Add pancetta and sauté a few minutes more, stirring occasionally. Add tomatoes, their juice, mushrooms, reserved liquid from mushrooms, salt and pepper. Simmer uncovered for 45 minutes. Stir occasionally.

Cook pasta until tender but firm. Drain. Put in warm serving bowl, pour sauce over pasta and mix. Serve immediately. Pass cheese to sprinkle on top.

* Available at specialty food stores.

# PASTA NIÇOISE WITH FRESH TUNA

SERVES 4

1   pound tubular pasta

Kosher or coarsely ground salt

1   tablespoon olive oil

1   (12 to 16-ounce) tuna steak

## TOMATO SAUCE

Grated peel of 2 large lemons

4   large red, ripe tomatoes,
    cored and quartered

3   garlic cloves, peeled

½   cup fresh basil leaves, stemmed,
    washed and patted dry

1   tablespoon capers, drained,
    washed and patted dry

16  small black olives (Kalamata
    or Italian), pitted

½   cup olive oil

3   tablespoons balsamic vinegar

Salt and freshly ground pepper to taste

Place sauce ingredients in the bowl of a food processor, and pulse on and off until roughly chopped. Alternatively, everything can be chopped by hand to a medium dice. Pour sauce into a bowl, cover and set aside until ready to use.

Cook pasta in 4-quarts boiling salted water for 10 to 12 minutes. While pasta cooks, place a heavy skillet over high heat and sprinkle pan with kosher salt. When salt begins to sputter, add tuna steak, sprinkle top of steak with more salt and cook until lightly charred, about 4 minutes. Turn over and cook other side 4 more minutes. The tuna will be rare. If you prefer it cooked longer, transfer to an ovenproof dish and bake in preheated 300° F. oven until opaque.

Transfer tuna to a cutting board. Drain pasta and toss with a tablespoon of olive oil.

Divide pasta among four dishes and top each with sauce. Slice tuna into ¼-inch slices and place over sauce. Serve immediately.

**Note:** *Tuna can be brushed with olive oil and grilled over hot coals, about 5 minutes per side for rare, as an alternative to the pan-frying method.*

174

# PASTA WITH RED PEPPER AND CARAMELIZED ONION SAUCE

SERVES 4

*The word succulent comes to mind.*

¼  cup olive oil

2  large Spanish onions, thinly sliced

2  red bell peppers, cut in ¼-inch strips

1  clove garlic, minced

½  cup dry white wine

¼  cup chopped fresh parsley

Salt and freshly ground pepper to taste

8  ounces of spinach-flavored pasta

Freshly grated Parmesan cheese

Heat oil in a large heavy skillet over very low heat and add onion. Cover and cook about 45 minutes. Uncover, raise heat to medium and cook until liquid evaporates and onions are golden.

Stir in peppers and cook, stirring, over medium heat until edges begin to brown, about 5 minutes. Stir in garlic and sauté another minute.

Add wine, raise heat to high and cook until wine is reduced to a syrup. Add parsley and season with salt and pepper.

Cook pasta until tender but firm. Drain. Toss sauce with hot pasta. Sprinkle with cheese and serve immediately. ❧

**Note:** *This is an excellent side dish or light main course.*

# Rigatoni with Vegetables

SERVES 6

1 pound rigatoni (or macaroni)

3 cups broccoli flowerettes

3 tablespoons olive oil

1 large red onion, chopped (1 cup)

1⅓ cups canned chickpeas (garbanzos), rinsed and drained

2 tablespoons minced garlic

2 cups diced canned plum tomatoes

Salt and freshly ground pepper to taste

Freshly grated Parmesan cheese

Cook rigatoni in boiling water until tender but firm; drain and set aside.

Blanch broccoli for about 2 to 3 minutes in boiling water until almost tender, then rinse in ice water to refresh.

Heat the olive oil in a large heavy skillet and sauté onion until it is soft. Add chickpeas and garlic and cook gently. Add tomatoes and broccoli and heat.

Stir in drained pasta; season with salt and pepper and serve, sprinkled with cheese.

# Linguine with Cabbage

SERVES 2

½ small head cabbage, julienned

4 tablespoons olive oil

½ cup chicken broth (homemade or canned)

1 teaspoon salt

Freshly ground pepper to taste

4 ounces linguine

¼ cup chopped scallions

3 tablespoons freshly grated Asiago or Parmesan cheese

Sauté cabbage in oil for about 5 minutes or until crisp-tender. Add broth, salt and pepper and cook about 3 more minutes.

Cook linguine until tender but firm. Drain. Toss with cabbage, sprinkle with scallions and grated cheese.

# FUSILLI WITH FRESH HERBS AND VEGETABLES

SERVES 4 TO 6

⅓  cup fresh lemon juice

Grated peel of 1 lemon

1  cup mixed fresh herbs such as tarragon,
   parsley, basil and thyme

½  cup olive oil, divided

1  large clove garlic, peeled

1  teaspoon salt

Freshly ground pepper

¼  cup capers (optional)

2  pounds of either asparagus, cut into
   bite-sized pieces, broccoli flowerettes,
   or julienned zucchini

1  pound fusilli (corkscrew-shaped pasta)

Freshly grated Parmesan or Asiago cheese

Combine lemon juice, peel, herbs, ¼ cup olive oil,
garlic, salt and pepper in a food processor or blender.
Chop to a rough paste. Move to a large serving bowl,
add capers and set aside.

Cook vegetable of choice until crisp-tender, drain and
add to bowl. Cook pasta until tender but firm, drain and
add to the bowl. Toss gently, adding more seasonings
if needed. If pasta seems dry, add remaining olive oil.
Pass cheese to sprinkle on top.

**Note:** This dish may be prepared in advance and served at
room temperature.

177

Rice
&
Pasta

# PASTA PRIMAVERA

SERVES 6

*Delicate, and not decadent, this verdant pasta deserves to be one of the rites of spring.*

4   tablespoons olive oil, divided

2   tablespoons pine nuts

1   cup thinly sliced fresh mushrooms

1   medium zucchini, split and sliced
    ⅛-inch thick

1   cup broccoli flowerettes

12  thin asparagus spears,
    cut in 1-inch pieces

½   teaspoon crushed red pepper flakes

½   cup frozen tiny peas

1   tablespoon minced garlic

3   basil leaves, finely chopped

4   ripe plum tomatoes, seeded and cut
    into ½-inch cubes

Salt and pepper to taste

1   pound spaghetti

2   tablespoons snipped chives

Whole basil leaves


## SAUCE

½   cup heavy cream

½ to ⅔ cup chicken broth
    (homemade or canned)

3   tablespoons sour cream

3   tablespoons unsalted butter

½   cup freshly grated Parmesan cheese,
    plus additional for table

Salt and freshly ground pepper to taste

Bring one gallon of water with 1 tablespoon of olive oil to a boil and hold on simmer until sauce is ready.

**To prepare sauce,** combine heavy cream, chicken broth, sour cream, butter, Parmesan cheese, salt and pepper in a 2-quart saucepan. Cook slowly over low heat for 5 minutes. Remove from heat and set aside.

In a large skillet heat 2 tablespoons of olive oil and toast the pine nuts over medium high heat until light brown. Add mushrooms, zucchini, broccoli, asparagus and red pepper and cook 5 to 6 minutes, stirring frequently. Add frozen peas and cook another minute. Season with salt and pepper.

Warm remaining tablespoon of olive oil in a small saucepan over medium heat. Add garlic and basil and cook slowly for 2 minutes; but do not let garlic brown. Add tomatoes, salt and pepper and cook another 3 minutes. Mix with sautéed vegetables.

Cook pasta, drain and return to pot. Add Parmesan cream sauce, chives and half the sautéed vegetables to pasta. If sauce seems too dry add more chicken broth.

Pour into a large warmed bowl and top with remaining vegetables. Garnish with whole basil leaves and serve with additional grated Parmesan cheese.

# RICH TOMATO SAUCE

MAKES 3 CUPS

*A smooth luxurious sauce for pasta.*

1 medium onion, chopped (½ cup)

1 carrot, diced

1 rib celery, diced

1 cup (2 sticks) butter, divided

4 pounds fresh plum tomatoes,
  cored and peeled (or 4 cups
  canned Italian tomatoes, cut up)

½ teaspoon salt

¼ teaspoon freshly ground pepper

¼ to ½ teaspoon crushed red pepper flakes

Freshly grated Parmesan cheese

In a heavy skillet or saucepan cook onion, carrot and celery in ½ cup butter for about 10 minutes, until onions are translucent. Add tomatoes and cook over medium-low heat for 30 to 40 minutes until sauce starts to thicken slightly.

Whisk remaining butter into sauce, a tablespoon at a time. Season with salt, pepper and red pepper flakes. Serve sauce over cooked pasta and sprinkle with Parmesan cheese.

179

**Rice
&
Pasta**

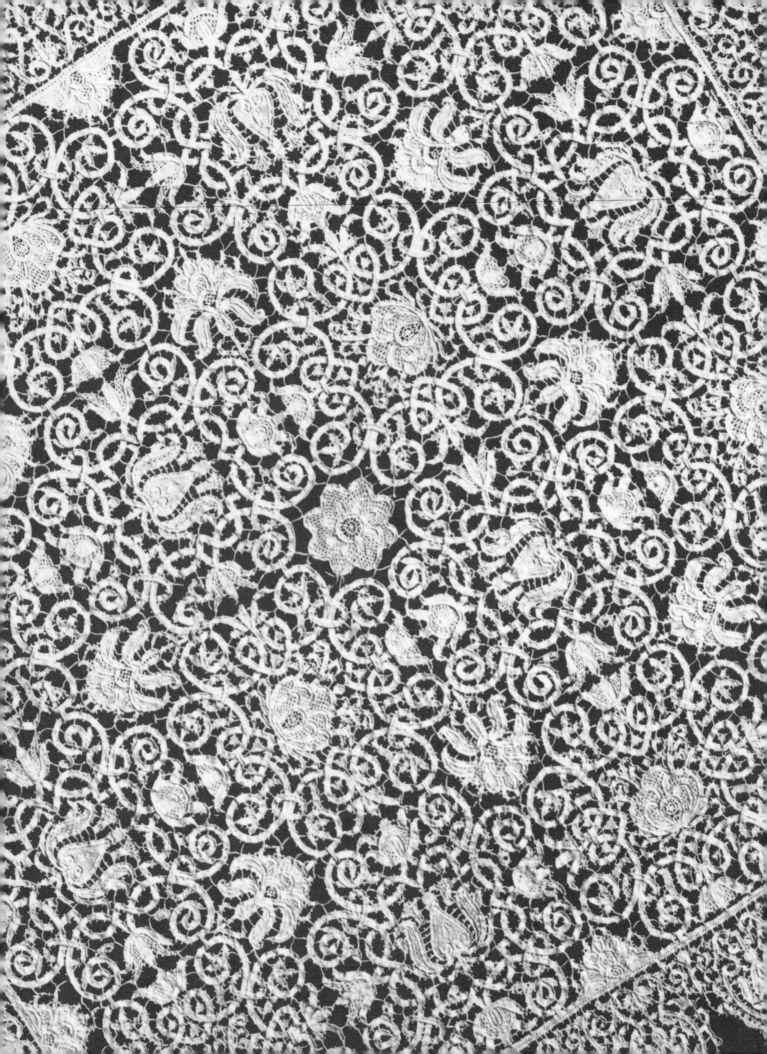

# DESSERTS

Detail from an early 17th century

Venetian lace chalice cover.

# APRICOT OATMEAL BARS

MAKES 32 BARS

1½ cups flour

1 teaspoon baking powder

½ teaspoon salt

1½ cups old-fashioned oats

1 cup firmly packed light brown sugar

¾ cup (1½ sticks) butter

1 (10-ounce) jar apricot preserves

Preheat oven to 350° F. In a medium bowl, sift together flour, baking powder and salt. Add oats, brown sugar and butter, cut into bits. Blend mixture until it becomes mealy.

Press half the mixture into a greased 8-inch square baking pan. Spread preserves over oat mixture with a spatula. Sprinkle remaining oat mixture on top and bake for 40 minutes or until golden brown. Cool, then cut into 2 x 1-inch bars. ✤

**Note:** *Vary the flavor by using other preserves — raspberry, strawberry — as desired.*

182

# ASBAR COOKIES

MAKES 3 DOZEN COOKIES

*The dough for these delicious "icebox" cookies may be prepared up to a week ahead and baked in batches as you wish.*

1 cup (2 sticks) butter

¼ cup dark molasses

1 cup firmly packed brown sugar (or ½ cup white sugar and ½ cup brown sugar)

⅛ teaspoon salt

1 egg

1 tablespoon almond extract

½ cup chopped almonds

¼ cup sesame seeds

½ cup raisins

1 cup oats

1¼ cup white flour

1 cup whole wheat flour

1 teaspoon baking powder

Cream butter with molasses, sugar and salt. Add egg and almond extract. Stir in almonds, sesame seeds, raisins, oats, flour and baking powder.

Mix until not sticky. Roll into logs and wrap in wax paper or plastic and refrigerate at least 2 hours. Preheat oven to 350° F.

Remove dough from refrigerator and cut into ¼-inch slices. Place slices on greased cookie sheets and bake for about 6 minutes. ✤

# ALMOND BRICKLE COOKIES

MAKES 2 DOZEN COOKIES

½ cup granulated sugar

½ cup confectioners' sugar

½ cup (1 stick) butter or margarine, softened

½ cup vegetable oil

½ teaspoon almond extract

1 egg

2¼ cups flour

½ teaspoon baking soda

½ teaspoon salt

½ teaspoon cream of tartar

1 cup coarsely chopped almonds

½ cup butter brickle or almond brickle baking chips

Granulated sugar

Preheat oven to 350° F. In a large bowl, combine sugars, butter, and oil. Add almond extract and egg and mix well.

Sift together flour, baking soda, salt and cream of tartar. Gradually add to creamed mixture, blending at low speed of electric mixer. Stir in almonds and brickle chips by hand.

Shape large tablespoonfuls of dough into balls, then roll balls in sugar. Place balls 5 inches apart on ungreased cookie sheets.

Dip a drinking glass in granulated sugar and flatten balls. Bake 12 to 18 minutes or until light golden brown around edges. Cool cookies for 1 minute before removing from cookie sheets. ❧

# LINZER BARS

MAKES ABOUT 40 BARS

1 cup (2 sticks) butter

2 eggs, separated

1¼ cups sugar, divided

2½ cups flour

1 (10-ounce) jar preserves, raspberry or apricot, warmed

1 cup semisweet chocolate bits

¼ teaspoon salt

2 cups finely chopped walnuts or pecans

Preheat oven to 350° F. Cream butter with egg yolks and ½ cup sugar. Add flour and knead. Spread dough on a greased, sided, cookie sheet to about ⅜-inch thickness (may not take up whole cookie sheet). Bake for 15 to 20 minutes until lightly browned.

Remove from oven, spread with warmed preserves and top with chocolate bits. Beat egg whites with salt until stiff, adding remaining sugar gradually. Fold in nuts. Spread over preserves and chocolate. Bake about 25 more minutes. Cut into squares or bars. ❧

**Note:** *To make a less sweet version of these delicious bars, decrease sugar to 1 cup and substitute unsweetened preserves.*

# BROWNIE SPOON CUPCAKES

(a favorite from the original *Artist in the Kitchen*)

MAKES 24 LARGE CUPCAKES OR 60 MINIATURES

*These extra sweet indulgences are back by popular demand.*

4   ounces semisweet chocolate

1   cup (2 sticks) butter

¼   teaspoon salt

1¾   cups sugar

1   cup sifted flour

4   eggs

1   tablespoon vanilla

### ICING

4   tablespoons (½ stick) butter

2   cups confectioners' sugar

Milk

Preheat oven to 325° F. In a double boiler, melt chocolate, butter and salt. Set aside.

In a large bowl, mix sugar, flour, eggs and vanilla. Blend in chocolate mixture and beat at medium speed no more than 2 minutes. Line cupcake tins with paper liners and fill each cup ⅔ full.

Bake for 25 minutes or less (15 minutes for miniature cupcakes). Cupcakes will fall a bit in the centers after they are removed from the oven.

While cupcakes are still warm, fill each center with a dab of icing made by creaming butter with confectioners' sugar and adding milk, a few drops at a time, until spreading consistency is reached.

**Note:** *Tastes like a brownie but looks much prettier! For a special occasion, use a pastry tube to fill centers.*

# SCOTTISH SHORTBREAD (a favorite from the original *Artist in the Kitchen*)

MAKES 24 PIECES

*An old-fashioned favorite that is so much tastier homemade.*

1   cup (2 sticks) butter, softened

½   cup sugar

2   cups flour

¼   teaspoon salt

Preheat oven to 300° F. Cream butter with sugar. Gradually add flour, kneading until smooth, at least 5 minutes.

Press into an 8 or 9-inch square pan to a thickness of about ½ inch. Pierce all over with a fork.

Bake for 10 minutes. Adjust oven to 275° F. and bake 1 hour. Cut into small rectangles while still hot.

# MAPLE WAFERS

*This simple cookie is delicious alone or serves as great company for a dish of ice cream or custard.*

¾   cup pure maple syrup

½   cup (1 stick) unsalted butter, plus 2 tablespoons

1   cup flour

2½  tablespoons sugar

¼   teaspoon baking soda

¼   teaspoon salt

1   egg

1¼  teaspoons vanilla

Preheat oven to 375° F. In a small saucepan over medium-high heat, bring maple syrup to boil. Boil 3½ minutes, or until syrup is reduced to about ½ cup.

Add butter and let mixture return to boil for 2 minutes. Remove from heat and let cool.

Sift together flour, sugar, baking soda and salt. Set aside. In a large bowl beat together egg and vanilla and stir in cooled maple mixture. Add dry ingredients and stir until well blended (mixture will be fluid).

Drop batter by small rounded teaspoonfuls about 3½ inches apart onto greased baking sheets. Bake 5 to 6 minutes or until wafers are gold-rimmed with ¼-inch of light brown. Watch carefully to avoid burning.

Remove from oven and let stand one minute. Then, using a spatula, quickly transfer wafers to wire racks before they become brittle. (If they firm up before they can be removed, return them to oven for 1 to 2 minutes to soften slightly.)

Cool baking sheets completely before reusing; grease thoroughly between batches. Store in an airtight container for up to 1 week, or in the freezer for up to a month.

185

*Desserts*

# SIENNA LACE

*Particularly at holiday time, these jewel-like confections are a welcome addition to the larder. They will improve in flavor if you can resist the temptation to consume them right away.*

2   ounces hazelnuts

2   ounces slivered almonds

½   cup (1 stick) unsalted butter

½   cup sugar

1   tablespoon flour

¼   teaspoon salt

2   teaspoons freshly grated lemon peel

2   teaspoons freshly grated orange peel

½   teaspoon cinnamon

¼   teaspoon nutmeg

⅛   teaspoon cloves

2   tablespoons milk

3½ ounces semisweet chocolate, melted

Preheat oven to 350° F. Toast and skin hazelnuts according to instructions on page 205. Toast almonds for about 5 minutes. Grind nuts in food processor or blender until fine. Set aside.

Line baking sheets with heavy-duty foil. Melt butter in a medium saucepan over medium heat. Add sugar, flour, salt, peels and spices. Stir until sugar dissolves, about 3 minutes. Mix in nuts and milk and cook until thickened, no longer than 3 minutes. Remove from heat and cool briefly.

Using a chilled spoon, drop by ½ teaspoonful onto foil, spacing 3½ to 4 inches apart (batter will really spread).

Bake cookies until deep medium brown, 8 to 10 minutes. Transfer foil, with cookies on it, to a rack or flat surface to cool completely. When cookies are cold, remove with spatula.

Wipe foil with paper towel and use again if desired. The cookies can be dropped onto foil sheets while waiting to bake.

When cool, spread underside of one cookie with melted chocolate. Sandwich with another cookie. They can also be served plain. ❧

**Note:** *To speed the dropping of the cookies and give a more uniform appearance, place batter in pastry bag fitted with a #4 plain tip. Pipe about the size of a dime. Do not let the batter become cold or it will be difficult to pipe.*

# STAR PEPPARKAKOR COOKIES

MAKES 4 TO 6 DOZEN COOKIES,
DEPENDING ON SIZE OF CUTTER

*A dark spicy cookie, delicious as is or decorated with icing. For an especially vivid enamel-like finish decorate with Jewel Yolk Paint.*

1   cup (2 sticks) butter, softened

1½  cups sugar

1   egg

2   tablespoons dark corn syrup

3½  cups flour

2   teaspoons baking soda

2½  teaspoons cinnamon

2½  teaspoons ground ginger

1   teaspoon ground cloves

½   teaspoon ground cardamom

Confectioners' sugar


JEWEL YOLK PAINT

2   egg yolks

¼   teaspoon water

Food coloring

In a large bowl cream butter and sugar. Beat in egg and corn syrup.

Sift together flour, baking soda and spices and add to butter mixture. Chill in refrigerator several hours or overnight.

Preheat oven to 350° F. Roll about ¼-inch thick on surface dusted with confectioners' sugar with a sheet of waxed paper placed over the dough.

Cut dough with star cookie cutter or other cutters. To make as Christmas ornament, cut hole in top of star cookie using a straw, before baking. Place on greased cookie sheets. Bake 10 to 15 minutes.

**TO MAKE JEWEL YOLK PAINT,** mix yolks and water and divide into small cups. Add different colors to each mix and paint on cookies with pastry brush before baking. ❧

# Tuiles*

*These crisp lacy cookie cups can form the base for many wonderful desserts. Fill with strawberries topped with whipped cream for a light dessert, or with chocolate, coffee or peach mousse for a richer presentation.*

2    eggs

2    egg whites

1    cup sugar

1    cup sliced almonds

¼    cup flour or matzo cake meal or cornstarch

½    teaspoon almond extract

Preheat oven to 400° F. Beat eggs and whites and mix with other ingredients.

Grease a heavy non-stick cookie sheet. Drop about 1½ tablespoons of dough on each end of the sheet. With the back of a spoon, spread the cookie in a 5 to 6 inch circle. Only 2 cookies will be baked at a time. Bake about 5 to 7 minutes.

When cookies are slightly brown at edges and a little brown all over, remove one cookie at a time and, with a potholder or paper towel, mold it over the bottom of a greased custard cup, roly-poly glass or whatever form you desire. Work quickly since tuile will become crisp and inflexible as it cools.

Remove from the mold. Continue with the remaining dough, baking and shaping 2 at a time. Cookie sheet may require additional oil.

To serve, place on a dessert plate and fill with mousse, berries or ice cream. ❧

**Note:**  *Store in an airtight container or freeze. In hot weather leave frozen until ready to serve.*

* Adapted from Frank Waldman

188

# Almond Butter Cake

SERVES 8

*This moist cake — wonderful alone — is especially tasty with a dollop of sweetened whipped cream and any kind of fresh berries on the side. It may be varied by adding the freshly grated peel of a lemon or an orange to the batter.*

10 ounces canned almond paste

1 cup sugar

10 tablespoons (1 stick plus 2 tablespoons) unsalted butter, at room temperature

4 eggs

¾ cup flour

½ teaspoon baking powder

Confectioners' sugar

Preheat oven to 350° F. Line bottom of a 9 x 1½-inch round cake pan with parchment or waxed paper and lightly butter paper. Set aside.

Place almond paste in a bowl and microwave 20 to 30 seconds to soften.

Add sugar and beat until almond paste is broken into small pieces. Add butter and beat until well mixed.

Add the eggs, one at a time, beating well after each addition and scraping bowl often. Add the flour and baking powder and mix well.

Pour into the prepared pan and bake for 45 minutes, until a tester comes out clean. Do not overbake. If top is sufficiently browned before cake is done, cover loosely with aluminum foil.

Cool in pan for 5 minutes, then turn out onto rack to cool. When cool, sprinkle with sifted confectioners' sugar.

**Note:** *For an especially pretty presentation, place a round doily on the cake before sprinkling the powdered sugar. Gently lift off the doily. A lacy pattern will remain.*

189

*Desserts*

# BLACKBERRY CAKE WITH LEMON ICING

(a favorite from the original *Artist in the Kitchen*)

SERVES 12

¾  cup (1½ sticks) butter

1  cup sugar

3  eggs, separated

1½ cups cake flour

¼  teaspoon salt

1  teaspoon baking soda

1  teaspoon nutmeg

1  teaspoon cinnamon

1  teaspoon allspice

3  tablespoons sour cream or buttermilk

1  cup blackberries, canned or frozen
   and drained, or fresh

1  teaspoon vanilla

### ICING

4  tablespoons (½ stick) butter

2  cups confectioners' sugar

2  tablespoons milk or water

2  tablespoons fresh lemon juice

*Freshly grated peel of 1 lemon*

Preheat oven to 350° F. In a large bowl, cream butter with sugar. Add egg yolks and beat.

Sift flour with salt, baking soda, nutmeg, cinnamon and allspice. Add to creamed mixture with sour cream.

Beat egg whites until stiff. Fold into batter with blackberries and vanilla. Pour batter into 2 greased and floured 9-inch round cake pans and bake for 25 to 30 minutes.

**TO MAKE ICING,** cream butter and sugar. Add milk and lemon juice. Add grated peel slowly and mix well. Frost cake when cool.

# PINEAPPLE CARROT CAKE

(a favorite from the original *Artist in the Kitchen*)

*This family favorite keeps beautifully and will satisfy a sweet tooth. It may be baked as a three-layer cake and frosted or prepared in a bundt pan and topped with a glaze.*

## CAKE

2   cups flour

1½ teaspoons baking soda

2   teaspoons baking powder

1½ teaspoons salt

2   teaspoons cinnamon

2   cups sugar

4   eggs

1½ cups oil

1½ cups grated carrots

½   cup finely diced celery

1   (8-ounce) can crushed pineapple, drained (or 1 cup fresh chopped pineapple)

½   cup chopped pecans

## ICING (FOR LAYER CAKE)

½   cup (1 stick) butter

½   teaspoon almond extract

1   (8-ounce) package cream cheese, softened

1   pound confectioners' sugar

## GLAZE (FOR BUNDT CAKE)

1   (10-ounce) jar apricot or peach spreadable fruit preserves

2   tablespoons Grand Marnier

Preheat oven to 350° F. Sift flour with baking soda, baking powder, salt, cinnamon and sugar.

In large bowl beat eggs and add oil, carrots, celery, pineapple and nuts. Add flour mixture and mix at medium speed about 2 minutes.

Grease and flour three 8-inch cake pans or one bundt pan. Pour batter into pans and bake 35 minutes for layer cakes or 50 to 60 minutes for bundt cake.

**TO MAKE ICING FOR LAYER CAKE,** cream butter and add almond extract, cream cheese and confectioners' sugar. Beat well. Spread icing between layers and on top of cake.

**TO MAKE GLAZE FOR BUNDT CAKE,** warm preserves gently in a saucepan. Add Grand Marnier and simmer until smooth. Pour warm glaze over cake.

191

*Desserts*

# CHOCOLATE MERINGUES

3   egg whites

3   cups confectioners' sugar

7   tablespoons baking cocoa

2   tablespoons flour or matzo cake meal

2   cups coarsely chopped pecans

1   teaspoon vanilla

Preheat oven to 350° F. Grease heavy cookie pans, or line them with parchment or waxed paper and grease paper well.

Beat egg whites until stiff but not dry. Add sugar, cocoa, flour, pecans and vanilla to egg whites. Mix well. Dough will be sticky. (Do not attempt to keep the whites inflated.)

Using about 1 to 1½ tablespoons of batter per cookie, drop them 2 inches apart on cookie sheet. Bake about 15 minutes. Allow cookies to rest on the pan a few minutes, then transfer to a rack to cool. When cool, store in an airtight container. ✦

**Note:** *These meringues freeze well. The recipe doubles easily.*

# EDELWEISS TORTE

*Not beautiful, this dessert is quick and delicious for a family treat.*

4   ounces German sweet chocolate

½   cup (1 stick) butter or margarine

3   eggs, beaten

1   cup sugar

½   cup flour

1   teaspoon vanilla

Whipped cream or ice cream

Preheat oven to 325° F. In a heavy saucepan over low heat, melt chocolate and butter, stirring gently. Cool.

In a large bowl, beat eggs until light and frothy. Gradually beat in sugar, flour and vanilla. Add chocolate mixture and blend well.

Turn into greased 9-inch pie pan. Bake for 30 minutes. Serve warm or cool with a dollop of whipped cream or scoop of ice cream. ✦

# CHOCOLATE RASPBERRY TRUFFLE TART

SERVES 8 TO 10

*A sliver of this very dense chocolate tart is a sophisticated finale for a special dinner.*

## CRUST

1¼ cups crushed chocolate wafers

⅓ cup, unsifted, confectioners' sugar

4 tablespoons (½ stick) butter, melted

## TRUFFLE FILLING

1 cup heavy cream

4 tablespoons (½ stick) butter

¼ cup sugar

10 ounces good quality semisweet chocolate, cut into small pieces

1 teaspoon vanilla

1 pint fresh raspberries

## WHIPPED CREAM (OPTIONAL)

1 cup heavy cream

2 tablespoons confectioners' sugar

1 teaspoon vanilla

Spray a 9 x ¾-inch tart pan with non-stick cooking spray. (Hold pan in sink while spraying.) Set aside.

Place crushed wafers in the bowl of a processor with confectioners' sugar. Process to make fine crumbs. Remove from bowl, add butter and toss with a fork to coat crumbs. Press into bottom and up sides of tart pan. Set aside.

TO MAKE FILLING, combine cream, butter and sugar in a heavy saucepan. Bring to a simmer and heat until butter is melted. Remove from heat and whisk in chocolate until melted. (Do not whisk too hard or air bubbles will form.) Add vanilla. Pour into tart pan. Chill slightly to partially set.

To assemble, starting at the outer edge of tart, place raspberries on top in concentric circles towards the center.

Serve in thin slices with whipped cream (beaten with confectioners' sugar and vanilla) on the side if desired. Makes one 9-inch tart. ✺

*Copyright 1992 by Helen S. Fletcher. All rights reserved.*

193

*Desserts*

# CHOCOLATE TORTE WITH AMARETTO CHOCOLATE SAUCE

SERVES 8 TO 10

*This is a dessert for chocolate lovers. Although there are several steps, the torte may be made early in the day while the sauce may be made several days in advance, refrigerated and warmed gently before serving.*

## TORTE

8   ounces (1½ cups) slivered almonds

1   cup sugar, divided

½   cup (1 stick) unsalted butter

6   ounces unsweetened chocolate, broken into pieces

5   eggs, separated

¼   teaspoon salt

1   tablespoon confectioners' sugar

## WHIPPED CREAM

1   cup heavy cream, chilled

2   tablespoons Amaretto (or other almond liqueur)

Preheat oven to 350° F. Butter a 9 x 2-inch round cake pan. Line bottom of pan with wax paper. Butter paper and set pan aside.

Spread out almonds in a baking pan and toast for about 10 minutes. Remove from oven, cool and grind them finely in a food processor with 1 tablespoon sugar. Set aside.

In a medium heat-proof bowl or double boiler combine butter, chocolate and ½ cup sugar. Place over 2 inches of simmering water until butter is melted and chocolate is soft, about 5 minutes. Remove from heat and stir until chocolate is melted and mixture is smooth, 2 to 3 minutes. Set aside to cool to room temperature.

Beat egg yolks into chocolate mixture one at a time until incorporated. Stir in ground almonds.

In a medium-sized bowl, beat egg whites with salt on high speed until stiff, adding remaining sugar 2 tablespoons at a time. Using a spatula, lightly fold egg whites into chocolate mixture, just until no white streaks remain.

Scrape batter into prepared cake pan and bake for 35 minutes, or until torte feels firm in the center when lightly pressed. Do not overcook. Let cool on a rack.

*continued next page*

194

## AMARETTO CHOCOLATE SAUCE

½  *cup heavy cream*

1  *cup sugar*

2  *ounces unsweetened chocolate*

2  *ounces good quality semisweet chocolate*

½  *cup (1 stick) unsalted butter*

2  *egg yolks*

1  *teaspoon vanilla*

3  *tablespoons Amaretto
   (or other almond liqueur)*

Run a thin knife around the sides of pan to loosen torte. Invert onto a rack and peel off wax paper. Set torte right-side up on a platter and sift confectioners' sugar evenly over top.

TO MAKE WHIPPED CREAM, beat heavy cream with almond liqueur until soft peaks form.

TO MAKE CHOCOLATE SAUCE, warm cream and sugar over medium heat in a heavy saucepan or double boiler until it simmers. Add chocolates and butter and cook over low heat, stirring, about 5 minutes. Remove from heat.

In a small bowl beat egg yolks. Gradually blend in 2 to 3 tablespoons of chocolate mixture. Pour egg mixture into saucepan with chocolate mixture and cook over low heat, stirring continuously, about 3 minutes.

Remove from heat. Stir in vanilla, and almond liqueur until blended. Makes 2 cups.

Serve torte at room temperature and pass chocolate sauce and bowl of whipped cream at the table. Or serve on individual plates from the kitchen; place a slice of the torte on a puddle of chocolate sauce and top with a dollop of whipped cream.

*195*

***Desserts***

# CRAVINGS DARK AND WHITE CHOCOLATE MOUSSE TART

## SERVES 12 TO 16

*This is a rich and beautiful dessert for a dinner party which can be prepared ahead. Each of the mousses may also be served individually on their own.*

### CRUST

½   cup hazelnuts, skinned

1½  cups flour

⅛   cup sugar

¾   cup (1½ sticks) butter, cut into pieces

2   tablespoons sour cream

### CHOCOLATE MOUSSE

12  ounces semisweet chocolate

1½  ounces unsweetened chocolate

1   tablespoon unflavored gelatin

3   tablespoons Cognac

3   egg yolks

1½  cups heavy cream

5   egg whites

**TO MAKE CRUST,** first prepare hazelnuts according to instructions on page 205.

Then combine flour, sugar, butter and hazelnuts in food processor until butter is in pea-size pieces. With processor running, add sour cream. Continue to process until dough forms a ball.

Remove and press into bottom and up sides of a greased 11-inch tart pan. Chill.

When firm, line with parchment and add weights (or dry beans or rice) to prevent crust from rising during baking. Bake in preheated 350° F. oven for 25 minutes.

Remove parchment and weights; return to oven for another 5 to 7 minutes until crust is dry and slightly browned. Let cool, then refrigerate to chill.

**Note:** *Crust may be made up to one week in advance and frozen until ready to bake.*

**TO MAKE CHOCOLATE MOUSSE,** in a double boiler over simmering water melt both chocolates.

In a small cup, mix gelatin and Cognac and place in a bowl of warm water to dissolve.

In a large heavy saucepan whip egg yolks until pale yellow and thick. Add heavy cream. Heat gently, stirring, until tiny bubbles form and remove from heat. Stir in gelatin/cognac mixture. Add chocolate. Stir until thoroughly blended.

In another bowl whip egg whites until soft peaks form. Fold whites into chocolate mixture until thoroughly blended. Transfer to storage container and chill.

**Note:** *Mousse must be made at least one day in advance and may be made up to a week ahead.*

*continued next page*

196

## WHITE CHOCOLATE MOUSSE

1  *pound white chocolate*

1  *tablespoon unflavored gelatin*

¼  *cup hot water*

1  *cup sugar*

¼  *cup water*

5  *egg whites*

2  *cups heavy cream*

TO MAKE WHITE CHOCOLATE MOUSSE, bring water in a double boiler to a boil and remove from heat. Place white chocolate in pan to melt.

In a small cup, dissolve gelatin in hot water and set aside.

In a heavy saucepan combine sugar and water. Stir to mix, then using a candy thermometer, heat to soft ball stage (215° F.).

Meanwhile, whip egg whites until soft peaks form. Add hot sugar syrup and continue mixing until cool. Do not stop mixer.

In another bowl whip heavy cream. Add dissolved gelatin to whipped cream. Add melted chocolate to cooled syrup/egg white mixture. Fold in whipped cream/gelatin mixture. Transfer to storage container and chill.

**Note:** *Mousse must be made at least one day in advance and may be made up to a week ahead.*

TO ASSEMBLE THE TART, use a separate spoon for each mousse, scooping a portion from each into cooked and cooled tart shell. Alternate between white and dark chocolate to make an interesting pattern or alternate white and dark chocolate in concentric circles. Chill. Serve with fresh strawberries. ⚜

*Copyright 1992 by Tim Brennan, Cravings Gourmet Desserts, Ltd.*

197

*Desserts*

# APPLE WITH DRIED CHERRIES

*This warm apple-cherry compote is especially good served with rich vanilla ice cream.*

1   apple, Jonathan, Pippin or other good
    baking apple

1   tablespoon butter, softened

2   tablespoons brown sugar

1   cup apple cider

½   cup dried cherries*

Peel apple, then cut it in half through stem and remove core. Spread both halves with softened butter, then coat butter with brown sugar.

Heat a non-stick pan (be sure it is one with a good-fitting cover) over medium heat and place the apples halved-and-buttered side down. Cook for about 10 minutes until crusty and brown, then turn apples over and add cider and cherries. Cover and cook over medium-low heat for about 15 minutes or until tender.

Remove the apples and cherries to individual serving dishes. Reduce cider to a few tablespoons by cooking it a few minutes longer uncovered over medium-high heat. Spoon cider over apples and cherries and serve warm.

**Note:** *Can be prepared ahead and warmed in oven or microwave.*

*\* Dried cherries are found in the produce section of most supermarkets.*

# APPLE CROUSTADE

SERVES 4 TO 6

*A dramatic presentation with minimal effort!*

2½ pounds tart green apples (about 5 large),
   such as Granny Smith

½  cup rum or Armagnac

½  cup (1 stick) unsalted butter, melted

½  pound (12 leaves) phyllo pastry*

½  cup finely ground almonds

½  cup sugar (or more depending on
   tartness of apple)

Confectioners' sugar

Peel, core and thinly slice apples. Soak in rum for at least 2 hours. Preheat oven to 375° F.

Brush a wide cake, pizza or pie pan with some of melted butter. Cover bottom of pan with a leaf of phyllo. Drape 7 more leaves onto the pan, brushing each with melted butter and sprinkling with ground almonds. One half of each of the leaves should extend beyond pan sides; the other half should cover bottom of pan. Arrange leaves around pan so that the entire bottom, sides and rim are covered.

Drain apples and place on pastry, sprinkling with sugar. Cover with 2 of remaining pastry leaves, brushing each with butter and folding in half. Fold extended leaves over top of pie to cover and enclose it. Brush top with butter.

Fold remaining 2 leaves in half and cut into 2-inch wide strips. Lightly brush each strip with butter. Loosely curl each strip and place on top of croustade in an attractive design. Drizzle on remaining butter.

Bake 20 minutes; lower oven to 325° F. and bake 20 minutes longer. When cool, dust with confectioners' sugar. Serve warm or cold. ✿

**Note:** *Full color photograph of Apple Croustade on page 16 shows Croustade with a serving removed—finished dessert will be fully enclosed in phyllo.*

* *Packages of phyllo pastry are found in the freezer section of most supermarkets.*

# APPLES BONNE FEMME

SERVES 6

*There is nothing better than a warm baked apple on a cool night.*

6 large firm cooking apples

12 tablespoons (1½ sticks) butter, approximately

6 slices white or wheat bread, cut in rounds

¾ cup sugar, approximately

½ cup Calvados (apple brandy), or dark rum

1 cup heavy cream

Ground nutmeg to taste

Preheat oven to 350° F. Core and then peel ⅓ way down each apple.

Melt about 4 tablespoons butter in heavy skillet and brown bread. Sprinkle each round generously with sugar.

In buttered baking dish, place an apple on each bread round and stuff apple with 1 tablespoon sugar and as much butter as core cavity will hold. Top with another tablespoon of sugar and pat of butter. Sprinkle with Calvados or brandy. Put in oven and baste every 15 minutes with juices in pan until apples are tender, but not mushy, 45 minutes to 1 hour. Serve warm with heavy cream, seasoned lightly with nutmeg.

# JENNY'S SWEDISH APPLE PIE

SERVES 6

*What makes this dessert different is the sweet, cookie-like crust. It melts in your mouth.*

**CRUST**

1¼ cups sugar

1¾ cups flour

1 cup (2 sticks) butter, softened

**FILLING**

4 to 6 green apples

2 tablespoons sugar (or more depending on tartness of the apples)

2 teaspoons cinnamon

Preheat oven to 375° F. Mix crust ingredients until blended. Divide dough in half and refrigerate one portion. Roll other portion to spread over bottom and sides of a 9 x 13-inch ungreased baking pan. Bake for 10 minutes.

Peel, core and thinly slice the apples. Sprinkle with cinnamon and sugar. Spread over baked crust.

Roll out remaining dough and cut into strips. Top apples with strips arranged in lattice design.

Bake for 30 minutes. Serve warm or at room temperature with vanilla ice cream.

# APPLE UPSIDE-DOWN TART

SERVES 6

*For a last minute dessert, substitute packaged refrigerated pie crust dough (found in dairy section of supermarket) for the pastry crust in this recipe.*

## PASTRY

⅔  cup flour

⅛  teaspoon salt

1  tablespoon sugar

6  tablespoons (¾ stick) butter, softened

1  egg yolk

1 to 2 tablespoons cold water

## FILLING

3  pounds cooking apples (about 6 large)

½  cup (1 stick) butter

⅓  cup sugar

**TO MAKE PASTRY,** combine flour with salt and sugar. Cut in butter with a pastry blender or work with your fingers. Add egg yolk and water, mixing until you obtain a smooth dough. Set aside for one hour.

**TO MAKE FILLING,** peel, core, and quarter apples. Arrange apple quarters to cover bottom of a 9-inch diameter ovenproof pan, or iron skillet. Add the butter, cut in pieces, between the apple quarters and sprinkle sugar over top. Sauté slowly on top of the stove for 30 to 40 minutes, stirring gently.

Preheat oven to 400° F. Roll out dough and cut it into a circle a little larger than pan. Remove pan from heat and cover apples with dough. Press down edges of dough inside rim of pan to seal in apples. Bake for about 20 minutes, remove from the oven, invert onto a serving platter, and serve either hot or warm.

# BAKED PEACHES WITH CARAMEL

SERVES 8

*The pure sweet flavor of ripe peaches makes this dessert a summer must.*

9   medium ripe peaches (about 2¼ pounds)

¾   cup sugar

½   cup heavy cream

2   teaspoons fresh lemon juice

Vanilla ice cream

**TO PREPARE THE PEACHES,** preheat oven to 375° F. In a large saucepan of boiling water blanch the peaches in batches for about 30 seconds. Remove and place in cold water to cool. Pat dry.

Peel, halve and pit peaches. Place all but 2 of peach halves cut-side down in a rectangular glass or ceramic baking dish and bake for 15 to 20 minutes until peaches are soft.

**TO MAKE THE CARAMEL,** slice remaining peach halves and cook in a saucepan over medium heat, stirring frequently, until very soft. Purée in a blender or food processor and set aside.

Boil the sugar and ¼ cup water in a heavy saucepan over medium-high heat. Stir once to dissolve sugar. Continue to boil without stirring until mixture turns a light brown, 5 to 8 minutes. Watch carefully. Do not burn.

Remove from heat and quickly blend in heavy cream, peach purée, and lemon juice to complete caramel sauce.

Serve peach halves warm or at room temperature topped with caramel sauce and a scoop of vanilla ice cream on the side. 

202

# FRUIT BUCKLE*

SERVES 4 TO 6

4  cups fresh berries (strawberries,
   blueberries, raspberries or a
   combination), or 8 cups sliced peaches

1  cup flour

1  cup sugar

1  teaspoon baking powder

1  egg

½  cup (1 stick) butter or margarine, melted

Ice cream or whipped cream

Preheat oven to 350° F. Place fruit in even layer in an
8 x 8-inch pan. Combine flour, sugar, baking powder
and egg and blend into a crumbly mixture. Sprinkle
evenly over the fruit. Pour melted butter over crumbs.
Bake until bubbly and golden brown, about 40 minutes.
Serve warm with ice cream or whipped cream.

**Note:** *This dessert looks pretty in individual ramekins.
Shorten baking time by about 10 minutes. Either way dish
can be prepared ahead and warmed just prior to serving.*

* Adapted from Bill Cardwell

# GRATIN OF FRUITS

SERVES 6

*This dessert is an incredibly easy yet impressive conclusion to a dinner with company.*

6  egg yolks

⅓  cup sugar

⅛ to ¼ cup liqueur, such as Grand Marnier
   or Framboise

3  tablespoons water

¼  cup heavy cream

3 to 4 cups fresh fruit such as peeled and
   sliced peaches, blueberries, plums,
   raspberries or strawberries

Sugar for sprinkling on top

In a double boiler over low heat, combine egg yolks,
sugar, liqueur and water. Beat constantly until sauce
coats a spoon thickly. Remove from heat and stir
in cream.

Arrange fruit decoratively in individual serving dishes.
Pour sauce on top and sprinkle with sugar.

Preheat broiler. Place fruit under broiler 1 to 2 minutes,
just until brown. Watch carefully so sauce does not
burn. Serve warm with a cookie on the side.

**Note:** *Sauce can be made early in the day and refrigerated
until ready to assemble.*

# CARAMEL BREAD PUDDING

(a favorite from the original *Artist in the Kitchen*)

SERVES 6

*One of the most popular desserts from the first Artist in the Kitchen and an on-going favorite.*

1    cup sugar, divided

4    cups milk, scalded

2    cups bread, cut in small cubes (not too dry)

2    eggs

½    teaspoon salt

1    teaspoon vanilla

*Whipped cream (optional)*

Preheat oven to 350° F. Put ½ cup sugar in a small heavy saucepan and cook over medium heat, stirring constantly, until melted and golden brown.

Add sugar to scalded milk and stir until dissolved. Pour over bread cubes and soak 30 minutes.

Beat eggs slightly; add remaining sugar, salt and vanilla. Stir mixture into soaked bread cubes. Bake in a buttered 2-quart casserole for about 1 hour, until slightly set and brown on top. Serve cool, with whipped cream if desired. ❧

**Note:** *Keeps well for several days in the refrigerator with no loss of flavor.*

# GINGER CHEESECAKE

SERVES 8 TO 10

*Fresh ginger provides a subtle tang to this creamy cheesecake.*

½    cup crushed gingersnaps

½    cup crushed chocolate wafers

⅓    cup melted butter

2    pounds cream cheese, at room temperature

½    cup heavy cream

4    eggs

1½   cups sugar

1    teaspoon vanilla

2    tablespoons grated fresh ginger

Preheat oven to 300° F. Grease inside of a high-sided 8-inch-diameter springform pan. Crush gingersnaps and chocolate wafers in a food processor or blender, or place in a plastic bag and roll. Mix with melted butter. Press crumbs into bottom and halfway up the sides of pan.

Place cream cheese, heavy cream, eggs, sugar, vanilla and grated ginger into bowl of an electric mixer. Beat until thoroughly blended and smooth.

Pour batter into pan. Bake for 1 hour and 40 minutes. At the end of that time, turn off oven and let cake sit in oven for an hour longer.

Place cake on rack to cool at least 2 hours before unmolding. Store in refrigerator. ❧

# HAZELNUT CHEESECAKE

*If cheesecake is your passion, you will be seduced by the luxurious flavor and texture of this toasted hazelnut entry.*

1½ cups (approximately one pound) shelled, toasted, skinned hazelnuts,* or blanched, toasted almonds

⅓ cup graham-cracker crumbs

2 pounds cream cheese, at room temperature

½ cup heavy cream

4 eggs

1¾ cups sugar

1 teaspoon vanilla

Preheat oven to 300° F. Place nuts in blender or food processor and blend briefly for a crunchy texture or longer for a smooth paste-like texture.

Butter the inside of an 8-inch springform pan. Sprinkle inside with graham-cracker crumbs and shake crumbs around bottom and sides until coated. Shake out excess crumbs and set aside.

Place cream cheese, cream, eggs, sugar and vanilla into bowl of an electric mixer. Start beating at low speed and, as ingredients blend, increase speed to high. Continue beating until thoroughly blended and smooth.

Add nuts and continue beating until thoroughly blended. Pour and scrape batter into prepared pan and shake gently to level mixture.

Set pan inside oven and bake 2 hours. At the end of that time, turn off oven and let cake sit in oven an hour longer.

Remove from oven and let cake stand on a rack at least 2 hours before removing from baking pan. Serve lukewarm or at room temperature. ❧

* To toast and skin hazelnuts, preheat oven to 350° F. Place hazelnuts in a single layer in a baking pan. Toast for 10 to 15 minutes, watching carefully, until they are lightly colored and the skins blister. Wrap nuts in a kitchen towel and let them steam for 1 minute. Rub nuts in the towel to remove the skins and let nuts cool.

205

*Desserts*

# PUMPKIN CHEESECAKE

SERVES 8 TO 12

*The gingersnap crust creates a striking contrast to the pale orange cheesecake and complements the pumpkin spice flavor.*

## CRUST

8   ounces packaged gingersnaps

¼   cup (½ stick) butter, melted

¼   teaspoon cinnamon

## FILLING

2   (8-ounce) packages cream cheese, at room temperature

¾   cup sugar

1   (16-ounce) can pumpkin

¼   teaspoon ground ginger

¼   teaspoon nutmeg

1   teaspoon cinnamon

2   eggs

1   teaspoon vanilla

## TOPPING

1   cup sour cream, at room temperature

1   tablespoon sugar

½   teaspoon vanilla

Crush cookies in food processor or blender or place in plastic bag and roll. Mix in butter and cinnamon. Pat into bottom of 9-inch springform pan. Chill.

Preheat oven to 350° F. In food processor or mixer blend ingredients for filling until very smooth.

Pour into pan lined with crumbs. Bake 50 to 60 minutes. Remove from oven.

Raise oven to 475° F. Combine sour cream with sugar and vanilla. Spread evenly on baked cheesecake. Bake for 5 minutes or until sides are bubbling and just barely beginning to color.

Cool on rack for 2 hours. Cover and refrigerate for at least 4 hours. Serve very cold. ❧

*Note: Very pretty decorated with chocolate leaves or other fall motifs. For a more exotic look use glossy pomegranate seeds or soft ripe persimmon slices.*

206

# FROZEN COFFEE MOUSSE WITH NUT BRITTLE

SERVES 4

## NUT BRITTLE

½ cup pecans or slivered almonds

⅓ cup sugar

3 tablespoons hot water

## FROZEN COFFEE MOUSSE

4 eggs

⅛ teaspoon salt

6 tablespoons sugar, divided

3 teaspoons instant powdered coffee

1 cup heavy cream

¼ teaspoon vanilla

2 tablespoons confectioners' sugar

## CHOCOLATE SAUCE (OPTIONAL)

5 ounces German sweet chocolate, broken into small pieces

5 tablespoons strong coffee

¼ cup water

3 tablespoons butter

**TO MAKE THE BRITTLE,** preheat oven to 350° F. Place nuts on cookie sheet and let them warm (but not brown) about 5 minutes in oven.

Meanwhile, put sugar into an iron skillet or saucepan and cook over medium heat until dissolved and golden. Turn off heat and carefully add the hot water and stir to dissolve. Immediately add warmed nuts. Stir over heat a few seconds and pour mixture onto a greased cookie sheet, spreading it out. Set aside to cool and harden. Then chop into small pieces.

**TO MAKE THE MOUSSE,** separate eggs, putting yolks into top of double boiler and the whites in a large bowl. Whip egg whites with salt, beating until frothy. Then beat in 2 tablespoons of sugar until stiff peaks form. Set aside.

Beat egg yolks with remaining sugar until they are a pale creamy yellow. Set over barely simmering water and continue to beat until thick and smooth. Add instant coffee, stirring to dissolve well. Remove from heat. Let cool at least 15 minutes. Stir in nut brittle.

Mix in ⅓ of egg whites to lighten mixture, then fold in the rest. In a separate bowl, whip cream and vanilla until almost firm, then beat in confectioners' sugar. Fold whipped cream into cold mousse mixture. Freeze at least 1 hour for a soft dessert, or overnight in metal bowl or decorative ice mold for a more ice-cream-like dessert.

**TO MAKE SAUCE,** stir chocolate with coffee and water over heat until smooth. Let cool to tepid. Add butter, by bits, stirring thoroughly to incorporate each piece before adding the next.

To serve the mousse, scoop into individual chilled dessert dishes on a pool of chocolate sauce, or if sufficiently frozen, unmold and serve as ice cream decorated with shaved chocolate or chocolate sauce. ৯৯৯

207

*Desserts*

# Maple Crème Brûlée

*A rich and flavorful alternative to a popular standard.*

2   cups heavy cream

1   cup pure maple syrup

6   egg yolks

6 to 8 tablespoons brown sugar

Preheat oven to 325° F. Mix cream and syrup in heavy saucepan. Warm over medium heat until slight wisp of steam rises. Do not boil.

In a medium bowl, whisk eggs and gradually add the warm cream whisking constantly. Pour all this into the saucepan and continue whisking over low heat until mixture is slightly thickened.

Pour into 6 custard cups or a 1½-quart baking or soufflé dish. Place in a pan filled with 1 inch of hot water. Bake for 45 minutes or until firm.

Chill for 3 to 4 hours. Sift 1 tablespoon brown sugar over each cup to cover surface. Place under broiler very briefly until sugar caramelizes. Be careful not to let sugar burn. Chill for at least 2 more hours. ❧

# Rice Pudding

SERVES 10 TO 12

*This is an authentic creamy Greek rice pudding. Chilling time is important for thickening.*

10  cups milk

1¼  cups sugar, divided

1   stick cinnamon

1   cup medium or short grain rice
    (River brand rice suggested)

3   eggs

2 to 4 tablespoons warm water

Ground cinnamon

Bring milk to boil in large saucepan. Add 1 cup sugar, stick cinnamon and rice and cook over low heat for about 45 minutes or until rice is soft. Remove from heat.

Beat together eggs, warm water and remaining sugar. Pour into milk mixture and cook over low heat until mixture boils gently and slightly thickens, about 15 minutes. Remove stick cinnamon.

Pour into glass or ceramic dish and sprinkle with ground cinnamon. Cool to room temperature then refrigerate for at least 2 hours. ❧

# LEMON CURD TART

SERVES 6 TO 8

## CRUST

9  ounces vanilla wafer cookies

⅓  cup confectioners' sugar

6  tablespoons (¾ stick) unsalted butter, melted

1½ teaspoons vanilla

## LEMON CURD

2  egg yolks

2  eggs

½  cup sugar

6  tablespoons fresh lemon juice

½  cup (1 stick) unsalted butter, cut into 6 pieces

## WHIPPED CREAM OR CHOCOLATE TOPPING (OPTIONAL)

2  ounces semisweet chocolate

1  cup heavy cream

3  tablespoons confectioners' sugar

1  teaspoon vanilla

Preheat oven to 350° F. Spray a 9 x ¾-inch tart pan with non-stick cooking spray. (Hold pan in sink while spraying.) Set aside. Crumb the cookies in a food processor or place in a plastic bag and roll. Mix in confectioners' sugar. Combine butter and vanilla and add to cookie crumbs. Stir lightly with a fork to moisten. Press crumbs evenly along sides and bottom of pan to make crust that is ¼-inch thick. (There may be extra crumbs.) Bake for 8 to 10 minutes until lightly browned. Cool completely.

TO MAKE LEMON CURD, place yolks and eggs in food processor and process until completely mixed. Pour into top of double boiler. Add sugar and lemon juice, stirring to mix completely. Add butter. Add very hot water to bottom of double boiler. Place top pan over (not in) water and bring water to a boil. Stir constantly until butter melts and curd gets very thick, about 170° F. on a thermometer. This only takes a few minutes. Do not overcook or curd will break. Pour into cooled crust and place plastic wrap on top of curd, smoothing out all air bubbles. Poke several holes in the plastic and let tart cool. Store in refrigerator.

TO MAKE CHOCOLATE TOPPING, melt semisweet chocolate in microwave at 50% power for 1½ to 2 minutes or in double boiler over low heat. Stir with a spoon until smooth. Dip spoon into chocolate and wave over tart in a back and forth motion to create a very fine chocolate pattern on top of tart. Store in refrigerator.

Alternatively, to finish tart with whipped cream stars, whip heavy cream until slightly thick. Add 3 tablespoons confectioners' sugar and 1 teaspoon vanilla continuing to whip until thick and cream holds its shape. Fit a pastry bag with a number 3 or 4 star tip and fill bag with cream. Start piping stars at outside edge and continue moving inward piping as many rows as you have cream. Some of tart should be exposed in center. Store in refrigerator. Makes one 9-inch tart.

209

*Desserts*

# PRALINE PUMPKIN PIE

*The praline topping adds a nice twist to a seasonal favorite.*

1    unbaked 9-inch pie crust

⅓    cup white sugar

⅓    cup firmly packed light brown sugar

¼    teaspoon salt

1½   teaspoons ground ginger

1½   teaspoons ground cinnamon

¾    teaspoon ground nutmeg

¼    teaspoon mace

⅛    teaspoon ground cloves

1½   cups cooked or canned
     unseasoned pumpkin

3    eggs, beaten

¾    cup heavy cream or evaporated milk

**PRALINE TOPPING**

½    cup firmly packed light brown sugar

¼    cup (½ stick) butter, softened

¾    cup pecans, chopped medium fine

Whipped cream

Preheat oven to 375° F. Prepare favorite pie crust or use recipe on page 32. Combine sugars, salt and spices in medium bowl. Blend in pumpkin and eggs. Stir in cream and pour into pie shell. Bake for 25 minutes.

**TO PREPARE PRALINE TOPPING,** blend together sugar, butter and pecans. Sprinkle over pie and bake an additional 30 minutes until filling is firm in center. Serve at room temperature with whipped cream.

# TIRAMISU

*The Italians named this rich coffee dessert "pick me up." Our Americanized version will provide a delicious lift to any dinner party.*

8   eggs, separated

⅔   cup sugar

1   cup Tia Maria (coffee liqueur), divided

1¼ cups Mascarpone cheese*

1   loaf pound cake, cut into ¼-inch slices, or 2 dozen lady fingers, split lengthwise

½   teaspoon instant espresso powder (not crystals)

Cocoa powder

Beat egg yolks with sugar and cook in double boiler over simmering water, stirring constantly until they become pale yellow.

Add 3 tablespoons Tia Maria and cook until thick enough to cover the back of a wooden spoon. Remove from heat.

Let cool slightly and beat in cheese with a wire whisk until smooth. Beat egg whites until stiff and fold into cheese mixture. In a 9 x 12-inch baking dish, spread ⅓ of cheese batter in bottom.

Combine remainder of Tia Maria with espresso powder. Dip pound cake slices (or lady finger halves) in Espresso/Tia Maria mixture until well soaked. Place pieces in pan holding batter until completely covered.

Cover cake layer with ⅓ of cheese batter. Repeat soaking and layering procedure for a second cake layer and finish with remaining ⅓ of cheese batter.

Sift cocoa powder over top. Chill for at least 1 hour before serving. ✿

*211*

*Desserts*

\* *Italian-style cream cheese, found in specialty food stores*

# ACKNOWLEDGEMENTS

Too many cooks may have spoiled that other cook's broth, but ours has only gotten better with their help. It is hard to imagine that a successful cookbook could be anything other than a collaborative effort; for most of us, good food and good company go hand in hand. We wish to thank the many people who have helped us — cooks, testers, and supporters alike.

Our category chiefs who took on the task of seeking out foods in the nine menu groups took great care to find recipes that were innovative, successful at first try, and tasty. Thanks to Patricia Hillis, Peggy Jones, Chip Reay, Jane Rouse, Linda Stein, Etta Taylor, and Susan Walter who have selected an interesting variety of recipes for each category.

Once the many recipes arrived, we turned to our group of testing coordinators to divide the recipes among the testers, to keep track of rave reviews versus criticisms, and to begin to hone their lists toward the final selection. We are grateful to Margaret Baldwin, Kathy Beilein, Ann Boon, Diane Burke, Hope Edison, Ellen Jones, Linda Langsdorf, Suzy Limberg, Betsy Markus, Jane Mitchell, Alice Muckerman, Liz Ruwitch, Julie Schnuck, and Sarah Thomasson for routing the recipes through various testers and tasters.

213

Like all good cooks, ours have been dedicated as well as adventurous. They contributed their time as well as the ingredients to experiment with foods and recipes on our behalf.

We thank . . .

| | | | |
|---|---|---|---|
| Margaret Baldwin | Patricia Hillis | Lisa Nouss | Rick Simoncelli |
| Virginia Bartling | Suzanne Hoffman | Sallie Painter | Liza Smith |
| Kathy Beilein | Sharon Hollander | Susan Patterson | Linda Stein |
| Ann Boon | Ellen Jones | Sofia Perry | Kate Stephens |
| Carol Brabbee | Peggy Jones | Cindy Peters | Etta Taylor |
| Loraine Budke | Mary Kelly | Joyce Porvaznik | Sarah Thomasson |
| Nora Buriks | Joan Langenberg | Bob Printz | Blair Thompson |
| Diane Burke | Linda Langsdorf | Chip Reay | Ruth Touhill |
| Phoebe Burke | Suzie Limberg | Jane Rouse | Marcia Trulaske |
| Marta Corrigan | Connie Lohr | Linda Ruesing | Gretchen Tucker |
| Kathy Cowhey | Betsy Markus | Mary Ruprecht | Liz Von Rohr |
| Jennifer Danielson | Barbara Messing | Liz Ruwitch | Carolyn Wagner |
| Hope Edison | Jane Mitchell | Julie Schnuck | Susan Walter |
| Dorothy Firestone | E.J. Moran | Sherida Schwarz | Amy Wartman |
| Lisa Fordyce | Mary Morgan | Gloria Sextro | Rita Wells |
| Cindy Grumney | Alice Muckerman | Lisa Shapiro | |
| | Janie Norberg | Nancy Sherman | |

It has been a pleasure to work closely with members of the Museum staff who have guided and helped us in moving this project forward. Special thanks to Rita Wells, the Museum's manager of retail sales, who has been the inspiration as well as the daily coordinator of this cookbook. Assistant Director Rick Simoncelli has been most helpful in removing obstacles from our paths, matching our ideas against realities, and moving us toward publication. Zoe Annis Perkins selected the textiles to illustrate the book. Debbie Boyer patiently typed the original manuscript and then revised it through its many refinements. Linda Ruesing tended to many details of coordination and communication that might have fallen through proverbial cracks had it not been for her vigilance. Mary Ann Steiner provided final proofreading.

Special thanks to Terry Mittelman, Blair Thompson and Kristine Brill who developed a plan for marketing and promoting the book and to Mark Erker and Helen Fletcher for their generous advice on its content. We are grateful to Amy Faulkenberry, John Vandover and Connie Fry of Obata Design, Inc. for their outstanding work in concepting, designing and producing this book and to Rich Murphy for photographing the textiles. Kudos also to Jon Bruton for his wonderful food photography and to Jackie Motooka, food stylist.

With gratitude . . .

214

**The Cookbook Committee**

Phoebe Burke       Mary Morgan

*Co-Chairmen*

Carol Brabbee       Dorothy Firestone

Lisa Nouss       Robert Printz       Jane Rouse

*Editors*

# RECIPE CONTRIBUTORS

Carole Bartnett

Kathy Beilein

Mary Bernstein

Marita Biggerstaff

Mary Black

Barbara Blair

Tony Bommarito

Ann Boon

Cynthia Bowman

Carol Brabbee

Katja Buckley

Loraine Budke

Diane Burke

Phoebe Burke

Nora Buriks

Mrs. D.O. Burst

Ron Denk, Catering St. Louis

Barbara Cook

Marta Corrigan

Kathy Poleman Cowhey

Ed Crader

Tim Brennan, Cravings

Susan Davidson

Patricia Degener

Mrs. John O. Dozier

Nicki Dwyer

Ilene Edison

Hope Edison

Mrs. Joseph C. Edwards

Dorothy Firestone

Bonnie Fisher

Helen Fletcher

Wesley Fordyce

Mrs. B.T. Forsyth

Betty Garber

Florence Goedde

Angie Golec

Margaret Grant

Sheila Griesedieck

Pat Hillis

Suzanne Hoffman

Irene Holmes

Linda Horsley-Nunley

Ellen Jones

Mrs. Frank Hyatt Kaiser

Thomas H. Kenton, Jr.

Yvonne Knobbe

Lea Koesterer

Barbara Krantz

Joan Langenberg

Pat Langenberg

Leslie Laskey

Sheri Lauter

Terry Lieberman

Suzie Limberg

Maureen Lorbert

Betsy Markus

Muffy Matthews

Ruth McBrayer

Lisa McMullin

Mrs. Sanford N. McDonnell

Jill Mead

Barbara Messing

Keithley Miller

Jane Mitchell

Mary Morgan

Joy Morris

Helen Moutrie

Alice Muckerman

Mrs. Albert C. Muehlman

Janie Norberg

Lisa Nouss

Mrs. Robert Orchard

Pane Caldo Bistro

Alice Pearson

Sofia Perry

Joan Pinson

Mrs. G.R. Pirrung

Bob Printz

Emily Pulitzer

Jennifer Pulitzer

Quatorze Bis Restaurant

Chip Reay

Liz Forrestal Reinus

Linda Ruesing

Ann Bradford Rhomberg

Audrey Rothbarth

Jane Rouse

Liz Ruwitch

Elsie Sadler

Jeannine Saye

Mr. and Mrs.
    Alexander Schonwald

Dorothy Schneider

Sherida Schwartz

Julia Scott

Audrey Shatz

Marsha Shepley

Liza Smith

Martine Smith

Louise Spitler

Linda Stein

Marion Stryker

Andi Sumner

Etta Taylor

Sarah Thomasson

Blair Thompson

Marcia Trulaske

Karen Uhlmann

Liz Von Rohr

Gail Walter

Susan Walter

Cassandra Weaver

Rita Wells

Amy Whitelaw

# INDEX

218

222

We hope you have enjoyed *The Artist In The Kitchen.*

Additional copies may be ordered from The Saint Louis Art Museum for $25.95 per book plus $5.00 shipping and handling. Please complete the following order form and return with your payment to:

*Museum Shop, The Saint Louis Art Museum*
*1 Fine Arts Drive, Forest Park*
*Saint Louis, Missouri  63110-1380*

or — call 314-721-0072 ext. 232 or 296 to place your order.

---

**I would like to order additional copies of *The Artist In The Kitchen.***

ORDER INFORMATION

| Number of Copies | Cost Each | $25.95 | Total |
|---|---|---|---|
| | Shipping (per book) | $5.00 | |
| | Grand Total | | |

METHOD OF PAYMENT
☐ Check  *(payable to Saint Louis Art Museum Shop)*       ☐ Visa    ☐ MasterCard

Credit Card Number _____     Expiration Date _____

Signature _____

ADDRESS
Name _____ Daytime Phone ( ) _____
Address _____
City _____ State _____ Zip _____

SHIPPING ADDRESS  *(if different from above)*
Name _____ Daytime Phone ( ) _____
Address _____
City _____ State _____ Zip _____
Gift Card Information _____

*Please allow 4 weeks for delivery.*

223

---

**I would like to order additional copies of *The Artist In The Kitchen.***

ORDER INFORMATION

| Number of Copies | Cost Each | $25.95 | Total |
|---|---|---|---|
| | Shipping (per book) | $5.00 | |
| | Grand Total | | |

METHOD OF PAYMENT
☐ Check  *(payable to Saint Louis Art Museum Shop)*       ☐ Visa    ☐ MasterCard

Credit Card Number _____     Expiration Date _____

Signature _____

ADDRESS
Name _____ Daytime Phone ( ) _____
Address _____
City _____ State _____ Zip _____

SHIPPING ADDRESS  *(if different from above)*
Name _____ Daytime Phone ( ) _____
Address _____
City _____ State _____ Zip _____
Gift Card Information _____

*Please allow 4 weeks for delivery.*

*Detach here*